# Praise

'I recognised so much in this book from my own experience. The approaches are practical, grounded, and real. A thoughtful, credible read for anyone who's been in the industry a while.'
— **Martin Traynor OBE, FIH**, Chair, Institute of Hospitality

'Cassie Davison captures the beating heart of hospitality – the people, the purpose, and the promise of belonging. *Stand Out Hospitality* is essential reading for anyone serious about leading with care and creating places people never want to leave. This book is one our industry has been waiting for. A thoughtful, actionable framework that reconnects leadership to empathy and excellence. Every independent operator should have a copy.'
— **Kris Hall MIH**, CEO and Founder, The Burnt Chef Project

'Cassie's belief in the power of hospitality to transform lives is like fuel for those who need to believe it too.'
— **Josh Shirtcliffe**, Manager, Cafe Fifty Five

'Part history lesson, part business advice, part love letter to hospitality, this book is a must read to remind us why we do what we do and help us to do it better!'
— **Katy Moses**, Founder and Managing Director, KAM Insight

'I was hooked from start to finish. *Stand Out Hospitality* is insightful, thought-provoking, and refreshingly practical. I took away so many ideas I can apply straight to our Airbnbs.'
— **Victoria Wood**, Fractional Marketing Manager, Her AI Edge

'Bold, honest, and full of heart. It felt like sitting down for a proper chat with someone who just gets it. The personal stories hit hard, and the way Cassie names burnout, doubt, and the messy bits no one else talks about is genuinely powerful.'
— **Gareth Hazad**, Co-founder, Why Hospitality

'Sometimes the universe brings you the people bearing the kind message you need to hear at just the right moment.'
— **Kieron Bailey**, Founder, People on Purpose

# STAND OUT

## HOSPITALITY

### HOW TO HAVE A BUSINESS YOU LOVE – **THAT LOVES YOU BACK**

CASSIE DAVISON

# Rethink

First published in Great Britain in 2025
by Rethink Press (www.rethinkpress.com)

© Copyright Cassie Davison

All rights reserved. No part of this publication may be reproduced, stored in or introduced into a retrieval system, or transmitted, in any form, or by any means (electronic, mechanical, photocopying, recording or otherwise) without the prior written permission of the publisher.

The right of Cassie Davison to be identified as the author of this work has been asserted by her in accordance with the Copyright, Designs and Patents Act 1988.

This book is sold subject to the condition that it shall not, by way of trade or otherwise, be lent, resold, hired out, or otherwise circulated without the publisher's prior consent in any form of binding or cover other than that in which it is published and without a similar condition including this condition being imposed on the subsequent purchaser.

Cover image © Shutterstock | janniwet

*To Robert, Florence, Jack, and Penelope.*
*May you always find the places you belong.*

# Contents

| | |
|---|---|
| Foreword | 1 |
| Introduction | 3 |
|     Why is this book different? | 5 |
|     The Five Pillars of Stand Out Hospitality | 6 |
|     How to use this book | 7 |
| **PART ONE   Where We Belong** | **9** |
| **1  Why Hospitality Will Always Matter** | **11** |
|     More than food and drink | 16 |
|     The third place | 19 |
|     Where the magic begins | 20 |
|     Summary | 26 |
| **2  Core Challenges And Customers** | **29** |
|     Three core challenges | 32 |
|     Customers | 33 |
|     How to win customers back | 39 |
|     Summary | 40 |

| | | |
|---|---|---|
| **3** | **The Team That Holds It All Together** | **43** |
| | A new generation, a new standard | 47 |
| | Summary | 53 |
| **4** | **Overwhelm: The Weight We Carry** | **55** |
| | The cost of carrying it all | 58 |
| | Seven common mistakes operators make (and what thriving businesses do instead) | 62 |
| | Summary | 68 |

**PART TWO   The Five Pillars: A Framework For Stand Out Hospitality** — **71**

| | | |
|---|---|---|
| **5** | **Set High Standards** | **73** |
| | The invisible weight we carry | 75 |
| | Pride, not perfection | 79 |
| | Protect what matters | 82 |
| | Surround yourself with excellence | 84 |
| | Summary | 87 |
| **6** | **Stand Out** | **89** |
| | When the noise takes over | 90 |
| | The risk of becoming 'just another' | 90 |
| | The room of ten | 91 |
| | Say no to the noise | 93 |

| | |
|---|---|
| Strategic clarity over mass appeal | 95 |
| Even I've been *that* customer | 98 |
| When business partnerships drift | 100 |
| Summary | 104 |

## 7 Define Your Identity — 107

| | |
|---|---|
| Start with purpose | 108 |
| Clarify your vision | 111 |
| Define your mission | 112 |
| Clarify your values | 116 |
| Design your customers | 116 |
| Let your values lead | 119 |
| Build from alignment | 120 |
| Summary | 122 |

## 8 Build Belonging — 125

| | |
|---|---|
| When everything clicks | 127 |
| When the team doesn't belong | 132 |
| Let go to make space | 134 |
| Not all customers are equal: Understanding loyalty | 136 |
| Summary | 143 |

## 9 Tell A Great Story — 145

| | |
|---|---|
| Hospitality is a story bank | 147 |

| | |
|---|---|
| Marketing that misses the point | 149 |
| Give customers a story to tell | 151 |
| Stories spread by people | 152 |
| People buy from people | 156 |
| The ripple effect of storytelling | 159 |
| Summary | 160 |

**PART THREE  Make It Last**     **163**

**10 Sustainable By Design**     **165**

| | |
|---|---|
| Unsustainable growth | 167 |
| Sustainable success means paying yourself first | 170 |
| When I didn't listen | 172 |
| The superpower that became my kryptonite | 174 |
| Rebuilding from the inside out | 175 |
| Self-compassion is strategy | 177 |
| You've built the framework, now live it | 179 |
| It takes a village | 181 |
| Summary | 182 |

**Conclusion: Let It Be You**     **185**

| | |
|---|---|
| Start where you are | 185 |
| The world we're building | 191 |
| Why chains still dominate | 192 |

| | |
|---|---|
| Why independents can win | 193 |
| Before you go | 195 |
| **Next Steps** | **199** |
| **Notes** | **201** |
| **Further Reading** | **205** |
| **Acknowledgements** | **207** |
| **The Author** | **211** |

# Foreword

I have known Cassie for over twenty-five years, since the very early days when she worked for me in my pub while setting up her first business. From the start, it was clear she wasn't just another member of staff. She had a drive and determination that stood out, even then.

Over the years, we've remained friends because of our deep passion for this beautiful, maddening, wonderful industry, but also because of who Cassie is. She is loyal, brave, and generous, with a resilience that has carried her through both the ecstatic highs and the brutal lows of running her own businesses. She never hides those realities, and that honesty is exactly what you'll find in this book.

When I read *Stand Out Hospitality*, it totally fired me up. It's not just for people in hospitality; it's a book about humans, told through the lens of the industry. It reminded me of things I'd forgotten and taught me things I didn't know. Everyone should read it, no matter what side of the bar they're on.

This book captures Cassie's experience, her courage, and her unwavering belief in what hospitality can and should be. It's written by someone who has walked the walk, and who still believes, after everything, that this industry is worth fighting for. If you care about people, purpose, and building something that matters, then you'll find yourself in these pages too.

**Dana Hunter**
Independent operator

# Introduction

This book is about the hospitality industry, but more specifically, it's about the reality of running an independent hospitality business today.

If you're here, it's because you've built something real – a pub, restaurant, bar, street-food truck, boutique hotel, coffee shop – and maybe even poured your soul into a handful of places. You're the one with the vision. The one who fixes what breaks, leads the team, and keeps the whole thing moving. You've weathered storms most people wouldn't understand. And whether your business is thriving or just staying afloat, you can feel it – something's shifted.

Margins are tighter. Customers are different. Teams are harder to build, and even harder to keep. While the old ways of working don't deliver as they used to, the pressure hasn't eased. If anything, it's increased. You're still standing. But if you're honest, it doesn't feel like it once did. The business might be doing fine – even well – but the joy, the momentum, the clarity? They're harder to find.

That doesn't mean you're failing or falling behind. It means you're living through one of the most complex, high-pressure chapters this industry has ever faced. You're not alone. What you're feeling isn't a flaw in your leadership – it's a by-product of a business model that demands a lot and rarely gives space to pause, reassess, or adapt on your own terms. That's what this book is here for.

Its framework, grounded in lived experience, helps you find a clearer, simpler, and more sustainable way forwards. An approach that helps you get clear on who you are and what you stand for, build loyalty that lasts, lead your team without losing your head, tell a story that cuts through the noise, and raise your standards without raising your stress.

I'm Cassie, and I've spent over thirty years in hospitality building, running, and growing independent venues from the ground up. I've won awards, earned an MBA, and led teams through everything from big wins to brutal losses. I've hit burnout, lost businesses, and rebuilt more than once. This book isn't theory, and it's not corporate advice dressed up for small businesses. It's what I've learned by living it. Independent hospitality still matters, and the people who run it deserve better than burnout.

## Why is this book different?

There's no shortage of advice out there, especially from people who've built empires or led large teams with big budgets. Their stories may be impressive, but they don't always reflect the daily reality of independent hospitality.

When you're running a small team, doing five jobs at once, and trying to make every penny count, corporate playbooks don't always translate. This book is different because it's tailored for you, the independent operator doing extraordinary things with limited resources. It's for those building businesses that are personal, values-led, and deeply rooted in their communities.

You won't find jargon here. No empty strategies or generic advice. Instead, you'll benefit from a grounded framework that helps you lead with more confidence, clarity and calm, enabling you to build something that feels good to run, not just impressive on paper.

I wrote this book because I've been where you are. I've built thriving businesses, and I've also lost everything. I know what it means to care deeply and still feel like it's not enough. To carry the weight alone. To wonder how much longer you can keep going. I also know this: there is a better way. This book isn't about doing more; it's about doing things differently. Simplifying. Reconnecting. Focusing on what matters most.

It's here to help you regain direction and control. To step out of survival mode and build something meaningful, with less stress, more direction, and a deeper sense of purpose.

## The Five Pillars of Stand Out Hospitality

At the heart of this book is a simple but powerful framework: the Five Pillars of Stand Out Hospitality. They aren't steps to follow or boxes to tick. They're tools to help you focus, simplify, and lead well, whether you're rebuilding, growing, or just trying to stay steady.

1. **Set High Standards:** Lead with consistency, clarity, and care.

2. **Stand Out:** Tune out the noise. Own your niche. Be unforgettable to the right people.

3. **Define Your Identity:** Be purpose driven. Know who you are and whom you serve.

4. **Build Belonging:** Create strong emotional connections with your customers and team.

5. **Tell A Great Story:** Share your 'why'. Let people in. Use storytelling to build visibility, trust, and loyalty.

These pillars are the foundations of thriving independent hospitality businesses, ones that stay strong, connected, and true to themselves when the pressure's on.

## How to use this book

This book isn't a course or a checklist. It's a guide.

You might be feeling overwhelmed. You might be standing at a crossroads. You might just need a fresh perspective. Wherever you are, this book will meet you there. Each part is designed to help you reconnect with your purpose, reset your direction, and re-energise the way you lead.

Part One reminds you why hospitality still matters and why you matter too. It explores the real challenges you're facing with customers, staff, and leadership. Part Two introduces the Five Pillars and shows you how to apply them. Part Three focuses on you – your energy, your leadership, and the sustainable success you deserve.

You don't need to read it all at once, nor do you need to implement everything straight away. Dip in and out as needed. Use the stories, prompts, and examples to reconnect with your intent and find your next step. Come back to it when things feel noisy. This isn't about more hustle. It's about building something that feels good to run and gives you a sense of belonging.

Let's begin.

# PART ONE
## WHERE WE BELONG

# PART ONE
## WHERE WE BELONG

ONE

# Why Hospitality Will Always Matter

Let's start by reminding ourselves why the hospitality industry is so important and special. Let's look at its place in history, society, and its significance to the health and functioning of our communities, relationships, and personal wellbeing.

It's easy to imagine how an industry like ours began – serving food and drink to travellers and offering rest to those on the move. For centuries, pubs, inns, and coffeehouses have met practical needs while also shaping our culture and connection. But the kind of leisure-driven hospitality we recognise today really began to accelerate in the modern era.

When Thomas Cook organised his first package tour from Leicester to Loughborough in 1841 (often credited as the beginning of modern tourism), it marked a shift.[1] Travel became something people did for pleasure, not just necessity. With that came new expectations of hospitality that were shaped increasingly around experience, comfort, and personal preference.

While selling food and drink has always had its place, the hospitality industry we know today is built on something deeper: the human need to belong, connect, and contribute. Nowhere is that more obvious than in the places we return to time and again. In the UK, there are two enduring touchpoints: the pub and the coffee shop.

Let's start with the pub, because to understand its role today, we need to remember the purpose it has historically served. The Porch House in Stow-on-the-Wold is often cited as being England's oldest inn, with parts of the building reputedly dating back to AD 947.[2] While this specific claim can't be verified – and we know that places to eat and drink predate even then – it's a powerful reminder that, for over a thousand years, we've gathered in places like this. To share stories. To celebrate milestones. To find comfort, understanding, and community.

Like the local restaurant, the corner café, or the small hotel, the pub isn't just a business; it's a cultural cornerstone. A place where life unfolds. There's a reason we call it the 'Great British pub'. Our society has been shaped around it.

## WHY HOSPITALITY WILL ALWAYS MATTER

Pubs were originally built to meet the everyday needs of communities. Some were alehouses – someone's home where locals could stop in for a drink and some company. Others acted as inns for travellers, with stables for horses, warm fires, and a place to sleep. Many were built near markets, docks, or along trade routes, serving as hubs where farmers, merchants, and labourers gathered to trade goods, hear the news, or find work. Pubs were used as meeting rooms, makeshift post offices, places of entertainment, and even venues for legal hearings and parish decisions. Practical, functional, and full of character, they were the backbone of local life.

They've always been places where people came together, often with a shared experience. Those who worked the land or the mills, those who travelled similar roads, or locals ending their shift or celebrating a win. Different backgrounds, the same need for connection. The pub offered that. It was a place where status fell away and hierarchy didn't matter. The lord and the labourer could stand shoulder to shoulder at the bar; equals for the time they shared the space.

The same goes for coffee shops, which date back to 1652 when Pasqua Rosée opened the first coffeehouse in London's St Michael's Alley.[3] Like pubs, they hold a long and important place in our cultural history, but they offer a different kind of gathering space. Originally emerging in times when abstinence and temperance were encouraged, they were in many ways the anti-pub – sober, social spaces where people could gather without the expectations or behaviours often associated with alcohol. At a time when images like artist William Hogarth's painting *Gin Lane* portrayed a bleak picture of public drunkenness and social decline, coffeehouses offered something different: a space free from societal pressure, where people from all walks of life could come together, share ideas, and exchange experiences.

Coffeehouses became hotbeds for innovation, discussion, and even revolution. In seventeenth and eighteenth-century Britain, coffeehouses were places of lively debate, political discourse, and intellectual exchange. They earned the nickname 'the penny university' because, for the price of a single coffee, anyone could listen as scholars, philosophers, merchants, and thinkers discussed the issues of the day. There were no formal lectures, no tickets needed – just curiosity, conversation, and caffeine.

Ideas that shaped society were fuelled over simple wooden tables and cups of coffee. Political movements such as the Levellers, early democratic thinking, and the free press found oxygen in these spaces. Coffeehouses became meeting places for writers, campaigners, scientists, and businessmen. In fact, several major institutions – including the London Stock Exchange, Lloyd's of London, and even the Royal Society – can trace their roots back to coffeehouse culture.

At their hearts, pubs and coffee shops have always been about belonging – places where people could feel at home, whether they were local or passing through. These spaces were built on human connection. Offering more than rest or refreshment, they brought people together, creating moments of companionship, shared stories, and collective experience. These venues were also spaces of innovation and social change. Culturally, they shaped the rhythm of daily life, becoming the beating heart of their communities. Beyond all that, they simply served a purpose – offering warmth, shelter, sustenance, work, and news from the world outside.

These venues were built to serve and, in doing so, they built something far greater: the very fabric of our shared lives. So, it's no wonder that during the 2020 pandemic lockdown, once the initial shock had settled and we'd made sure our loved ones were safe, the first thing many of us missed was our hospitality venues. No wonder that, when they tentatively reopened, we queued up to get a drink from the bar or sit in a pub garden with friends. We'd had access to supermarkets the whole time, so it was never about the drink. It was about something deeper. The need to feel normal again. To reconnect with the spaces that made us feel human. To know that those places – the ones that quietly hold our lives together – were still there. These places matter to us, often for reasons we can't fully explain.

## More than food and drink

Abraham Maslow developed his Hierarchy of Needs in 1943 as a psychological theory to explain human motivation and behaviour.[4] He proposed that people are driven by a set of needs, arranged in a hierarchy, starting with the most basic survival and moving towards more complex emotional and psychological needs. The idea is that lower-level needs must be at least partly satisfied before individuals can focus on the higher-level needs.

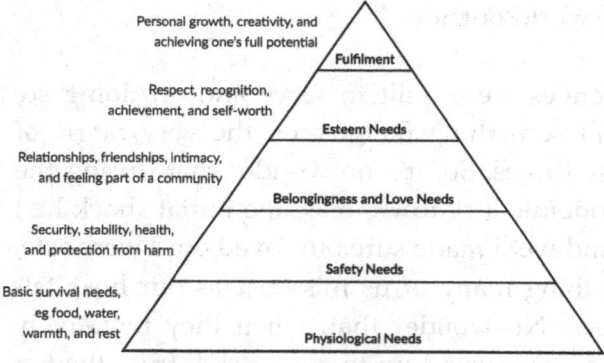

*Maslow's Hierarchy of Needs*

The five levels are:

- **Physiological:** Basic survival needs like food, water, warmth, and rest.
- **Safety:** Security, stability, health, and protection from harm.

- **Belongingness and love:** Relationships, friendships, intimacy, and feeling part of a community.
- **Esteem:** Respect, recognition, achievement, and self-worth.
- **Self-actualisation:** Fulfilment, personal growth, creativity, and achieving one's full potential.

Maslow believed that human behaviour is largely shaped by where a person is within this hierarchy. Once basic needs are met, we begin to seek deeper, more meaningful experiences and connections.

In today's world, where food and drink are abundant and easily accessible, hospitality is no longer about satisfying our most basic needs. We don't go to restaurants because we're starving or stay in a hotel simply for shelter. Those physiological and safety needs are already met. What people are really seeking, often without even realising it, is something higher up Maslow's hierarchy: belonging, connection, recognition, joy, and inspiration. Fulfilling these is the true role of hospitality today.

When someone walks through our doors, it's not just about what's on the plate or in the glass – it's about how we make them feel. As Will Guidara, author of *Unreasonable Hospitality* and a leading voice in modern service culture, explains: 'Service is black and white; hospitality is color.'[5] We're not in the business of transactions; we're in the business of transformation. We don't just serve food and drink, we create moments of meaning, warmth, and human connection. That's what makes hospitality essential, not just for our economy, but for our collective wellbeing, sense of community, and ability to truly feel like we belong.

This idea is echoed in the work of Tony Robbins, one of the world's most influential voices on human behaviour and peak performance. A globally recognised life and business strategist, bestselling author, and coach to leaders, entrepreneurs, and change-makers for over four decades, Robbins has shaped how millions of people understand personal growth, leadership, and fulfilment. He identifies six core human needs that shape every decision we make: certainty, variety, significance, connection, growth, and contribution.[6]

When we look at hospitality through this lens, we realise something powerful: it is one of the few industries that can meet all six of these needs. A regular pub visit offers certainty and familiarity. A themed event or new menu brings variety. Being remembered by name or having your favourite drink ready speaks to significance. Gathering with friends, meeting someone new, or simply being seen and welcomed fulfils our need for connection. A thoughtful conversation over coffee can spark growth, and, at its best, everything we do in hospitality is an act of contribution.

Hospitality doesn't just sit at the bottom of the hierarchy of needs; it reaches all the way to the top. That's what makes our work so meaningful, and why it matters now more than ever.

## The third place

Sociologist Ray Oldenburg describes third places as the vital spaces in our lives outside of home (our first place) and work (our second place).[7] In our first and second places, we have roles to play: parent, child, partner, boss, employee, caregiver, host, guest. We are constantly showing up as someone and doing what's expected of us. In a third place, those roles soften. There's no expectation to perform. You can show up alone or with others. You can chat or sit quietly. Somehow, just by being there, you feel like you belong.

Every hospitality business is a third place. From the quiet corner of a café where someone gathers their thoughts to the familiar bar stool where a regular unwinds after a long day, these spaces offer something profoundly human: the freedom to simply be. That's the quiet power of hospitality. We create spaces where people can be fully themselves, even if they don't speak to anyone else. Where they recognise something in the people around them – a shared energy, rhythm, and feeling of home. A sense of tribe.

Hospitality, at its best, levels the playing field. It says, 'You're welcome here, just as you are.' We're not just offering food and drink; we're offering freedom, safety, and connection in a world that often asks people to wear masks and meet expectations. That's the magic. In hospitality, we aren't just serving customers – we're creating spaces where people are no longer defined by their job titles or family roles. Where they can pause, belong, and just be.

That's why third places matter. That's why what we do matters. And that's why hospitality, despite its challenges, is not only a vital part of society but also one of the most rewarding, human, and hopeful industries in the world.

## Where the magic begins

When I was a little girl, both of my parents worked full time. We'd come home from school to a tired and stressed-out mum, and dad would work late. Although I have happy memories of childhood, home life was sometimes strained due to the weight of everything that needed to be done for a busy family.

I always looked forward to the weekends, when my parents would meet up with friends. They seemed to be on a mission to visit every pub in the area. We went camping with the same circle of friends, winding our way through the countryside, as if there was

## WHY HOSPITALITY WILL ALWAYS MATTER

a map of every pub and we needed to tick off each one. Perhaps there was a map. Perhaps it was their collective hobby.

This was back when kids weren't always welcome in the main pub, and more often than not, we were confined to the skittle alley with a packet of crisps and a fizzy drink. In summer, we would spend our days exploring the pub gardens. Many also had rooms where kids could watch cartoons or play Connect Four.

What I remember most clearly wasn't the other children; it was watching my parents come alive with their friends. They joked, they argued, they were themselves. They had a tribe, and the pub was where that tribe came together to bond, share ideas, commiserate, laugh, celebrate, and feel seen and supported. The pub was the place where I saw my parents be their full selves. Even then, I knew that was the magic of hospitality, and I wanted to be part of it.

Our stories of how we fell in love with hospitality are often surprisingly similar. On the Kith & Kin podcast, I have the privilege of chatting with amazing people from across the industry. Every episode begins with the same question: 'What made you fall in love with hospitality?'

The answers usually reflect two broad groups. Like me, the first group had an early experience that opened their eyes to the magic of hospitality, witnessing adult relationships blossom in warm, welcoming spaces, and feeling the care and kindness of those serving. The purpose and joy found in creating moments and spaces for others stayed with them.

One podcast guest, Ines, shared a beautiful story of visiting a local restaurant as a child, staying up late, and soaking in the joy and sense of community. As Ines tells the story on the podcast, it gives me goosebumps. I can feel the emotion in her voice; I can picture the place, the people, the late nights, the joy, and warmth. That's the power of hospitality: these spaces become the backdrop to the memories that stay with us, the stories we tell, and the moments that shape who we are.

What struck Ines most was the restaurant owner. While everyone else relaxed, the owner seemed to relish the act of hosting even more. There was something deeply inspiring about watching someone find joy in making others feel seen, safe, and connected. That sense of contribution and of providing a social anchor for others is genuinely intoxicating for so many of us. In Ines's case, it's taken her on a rich, winding journey through a bold and ever-evolving career in hospitality.

There's no doubt that hospitality professionals are a caring bunch. Speak with anyone in the industry and you'll find empathy at their core. We're sensitive to criticism, not because we're fragile, but because we want to please. That sensitivity is a superpower. Our ability to empathise enables us to perform a beautiful act of service, intuiting what someone needs before they ask, anticipating every detail, and seeing and quietly removing obstacles before they arise.

Anyone who takes the time to watch hospitality professionals at the top of their game can witness the cogs turning. Every movement is intentional, every decision shaped by the imagined experience of the guest. It's why, more often than not, any harsh reviews can feel so unfair, because this work is about serving others, not just delivering a product.

For the second group, although they often share a similar story of an early experience as a hospitality customer, the moment they truly felt they belonged was when they first felt valued.

Many young people come into this industry filled with enthusiasm and a willingness to work hard, but in the past, they've been made to feel like failures. They couldn't sit still. They didn't settle in school. They've struggled. They've been told they wouldn't amount to much. The sheer number of hospitality professionals who have either been diagnosed with or suspect they have some form of neurodiversity is no surprise.

So, when someone enters a busy hospitality environment – often with no previous experience, and sometimes without a proper interview or induction – and they're made to feel useful from day one, it can be life-changing. Many of us started out as a pot wash. To those on the outside, it's seen as the lowest of the low: the most basic, unskilled job anyone could do. In the industry, we know just how untrue that is. In any café, restaurant, pub, or hotel, the pot wash is a vital cog in the wheel. Without them, everything collapses. Unless that person is on their game – fast, efficient, quietly getting on without needing to ask too many questions – then service falters. There's no point serving Michelin-standard food if it can't be presented on an immaculate plate. A busy café can't deliver joy to waiting families without clean cups and matching saucers ready to go. A pub will grind to a halt without someone meticulously collecting, cleaning, and stacking glasses back on the shelves, all without getting in the way of customers or the besieged bar staff.

The sense of being needed and part of something can inspire loyalty and a deep sense of belonging from the very beginning, especially when you're not used to being seen or heard. Those of us who have built our careers in hospitality have found our home. We found where we belonged – our tribe, our people. We are inspired to be the best at what we do, not just for ourselves, but in service of others: our teams, customers, and communities.

And what better industry? Where else can you start with no previous work experience and be promoted to manager within two years? The opportunities in hospitality are endless. The learning you can gain from operations and serving others is second to none: customer service, problem solving, teamwork, leadership, crisis management, and it doesn't stop there. You also learn resilience, time management, communication under pressure, emotional intelligence, adaptability, and how to read people quickly and respond appropriately.

These are all transferable skills. I often tell the story of a friend who runs a creative agency. He once employed an eighteen-year-old with a YouTube channel that had over a million followers. He had no concerns about her ability in the role, except when it came to interacting with clients, networking in a room full of adults, and working as part of a team. He knew that, despite all the things he could teach her, some lessons could only be learned by doing. She needed to find her own way. So, he paid her to take a Saturday job in her local pub for six months. He was right – six months serving customers, and she learned how to do all of it. More than that, she built confidence.

The industry itself is full of opportunities. Many people don't necessarily go on to become a general manager, head chef, or run their own place. Plenty find their niche and move into other roles that suit them. There's no shortage of options, from marketing, systems, finance, HR, legal, and procurement, to learning and development, events and operations, technology and digital transformation, branding, sustainability, and guest experience management. The list goes on, and that's before even touching the wider hospitality ecosystem. It takes a village to keep a single business running: suppliers, maintenance teams, designers, builders, coaches, consultants, training providers, software developers, food producers, linen services, photographers, PR specialists, accountants, and more.

The paths are as varied as the people. What a fantastic industry – no wonder we love it.

## Summary

Hospitality has always been about more than food and drink. It's where life unfolds – where people connect, feel held, and return to what matters. In this chapter, we looked at the places that historically shaped our society – pubs, coffeehouses, inns – and how, for well over a thousand years, they've quietly held our communities together. These spaces were never merely venues; they were places where status evaporated, stories were shared, and people met as equals. They offered warmth, a welcome, and a sense of belonging.

We explored how hospitality today meets not only our basic needs, but also our deeper ones. It offers a place to feel welcome and understood; to be part of something, without needing to perform. That's why hospitality matters now more than ever.

You heard how many of us fell in love with hospitality at a young age, drawn in by a feeling we couldn't quite explain at the time. A moment of magic. A sense of tribe. A place where we felt valued, useful, and proud. Whether it started as a childhood memory or on a pot wash shift that changed everything, this industry gave us a place where we belong. It gave us confidence. Purpose. The chance to contribute.

That's an important point: hospitality isn't just where stories happen for our customers, it's where our stories begin, too. We don't just serve food and drink; we create moments that people remember and memories that hold meaning. We're not just in the service industry, we're in the business of belonging. And after a thousand years, that still matters. More than ever.

## TWO
# Core Challenges And Customers

Let's be real. Hospitality comes with significant challenges.

When I set the context for almost every conversation I have about this wonderful industry, I find myself repeating the same phrase: 'Hospitality is always in crisis.' That's not to dismiss the real – and often traumatic – challenges businesses have faced recently, especially in the aftermath of the pandemic. But throughout my thirty years in the industry, there has always been one thing after another.

For example, 9/11 changed how we approached our work and how customers behaved. We were told the smoking ban would be the end. Then came the 2007 economic crash, followed by years of austerity. At every budget announcement and new piece of legislation, we sit on the edge of our seats, waiting to work out what impact it will have on our businesses or our customers' behaviour.

The reality is hospitality sits at the coalface. Our industry is deeply exposed. We interact with customers directly, face-to-face, and we're the final point in the B2B chain. When the global economy shifts, even slight tremors further up the line can intensify by the time they reach us. What begins as a minor disruption becomes a major challenge, compounded by pressure from every link along the way. At the same time, feeling the same economic strain, customers start to spend less. By the time they hit our businesses, those small butterfly wing flaps have turned into tornadoes.

After decades in the industry, I've become much more pragmatic about these things. I remember once hearing a senior politician announce that there was no need to panic-buy petrol. I knew immediately that I might as well pack up shop for the week, because almost every one of my customers was promptly about to cancel, choosing instead to queue for petrol or conserve what they had. Stories like this remind us how something seemingly small can threaten your business or, at the very least, rob you of sleep. For those of you who have experienced it, I'm sure you carry the same scars.

Sometimes, it's simply nature that impacts us. I was in Brighton recently over the Easter bank holiday. It was

## CORE CHALLENGES AND CUSTOMERS

unseasonably hot, the sun was shining, every street was buzzing, and every venue's outside seating area was full. It felt like the height of summer. It was joyful to see such busy venues, and even more so to see people spending time with those who matter most. But I couldn't help thinking: if it had been cold, raining, or even snowing – as it sometimes does in April – the picture would have been very different. The unseasonable sunshine could have made or broken some of those businesses, and the true impact of a single day like that is rarely seen or easily quantified.

When you add the unpredictability of customer behaviour into the mix, it only gets harder. If you've spent any time running a venue, you'll know exactly what I mean. Throughout my thirty years, whether in restaurants, a city bar, a country pub, a café, or even festivals, it has been impossible to predict what people would do on a bank holiday. It often felt like the public had held a secret meeting and forgotten to invite us. Planning stock and staffing was always a gamble, one I never truly mastered, regardless of how much data I tracked. Yes, you could spot some patterns across the week, but those 'special days' never followed the rules. It's a bit like trying to predict a starling murmuration – beautiful to watch, impossible to control.

The reality is that running an independent hospitality business is notoriously hard. We're not large chains with the luxury of scale. We're small businesses, making high-stakes decisions in low-margin environments, with little room for error. As an owner-operator of a bricks-and-mortar venue, you're expected to know everything about an incredibly complex business. Set-up costs are high. You can't build slowly or test quietly; you have to get it right from the start. You're managing multiple functions at once: operations, finance, HR, marketing, compliance, and guest experience. Staffing costs are high, and recruiting and keeping good people are ongoing challenges. Customers are numerous, but attracting and retaining them demand constant marketing and deep loyalty-building. Margins are small, which means there's little room for mistakes or bad months.

It's a good thing I started this book by celebrating the positive side of the industry, because the nuts and bolts can feel a bit daunting. Hospitality comes with high risks – financial, operational, and emotional. It takes a rare kind of optimism to sign that lease, fit out that building, and open the doors, knowing that everything from the economy to the weather could be stacked against you. And there's no doubt that, right now, it's harder than ever for owner-operators to navigate these pressures.

## Three core challenges

To get a more in-depth understanding of how challenges impact independent operators day to day, we recently surveyed hospitality business owners as part of a benchmarking exercise to highlight the ninety-nine problems they're currently facing. Their answers made one thing clear: almost all the challenges they face fall into three main categories: customers, staff, and overwhelm.

Let's take a closer look at what those three core challenges mean on the ground. In this chapter, we'll discuss the first challenge: customers.

## Customers

Many operators highlight the challenge of getting customers through the door. Hospitality today is far more competitive than it has ever been. There are more venues, alternative ways to spend time, and people competing for the attention of our customers. It's not just a feeling; it's real.

When I opened my first venue in Leicester in 1999, licensing laws still restricted the number of places serving alcohol. Options for customers were limited to existing pubs or restaurants. The culture of 'city bars' was still new. It wasn't until the Licensing Act 2003 (enforced from 2005) that licensing eased, and a wave of new venues followed.[8] At that time, Leicester's West End had a few old pubs, a couple of restaurants, and just two bars. Ten years later, the area was packed shoulder to shoulder with hospitality venues – a brilliant explosion of choice for customers, but a much tougher environment for operators.

When you're one of a few, you can get away with a lot more. Standing out in a crowd demands a different approach, and that's without even mentioning competition from beyond hospitality. In 1999, if you wanted to stay home, your entertainment options were limited. There was always the option of a house party, but hosting one usually meant a lot of hard work and clearing up, depending on how well-behaved your guests were. As for home entertaining, most of us had Delia Smith's *Complete Cookery Course* on the shelf.[9] Dinner parties were planned well in advance, and it wasn't unusual to spend the whole day preparing to host friends properly. Gaming wasn't a thing for the older generations, and for the young, there were no online chats or multiplayer servers. If you wanted to socialise, it meant piling around to someone's house to watch one person play single-player on their PlayStation.

Going out was how we socialised, connected, and met our people. Back then, the choices were far more restricted, but the world has changed. These days, there are so many venues. Constant noise. As retail has slowed in our towns and cities, the antidote to empty units has often been a shift towards hospitality. There has been a wider trend too: a move from spending on 'stuff' to spending on experiences, with time spent with family and friends being among those.

## CORE CHALLENGES AND CUSTOMERS

Standing out on your own street, never mind across a town, city, or, for rural venues, an entire county, has become much harder. There are simply more venues competing for attention. There are also more ways than ever for customers to meet their needs without even leaving home. They can stream entertainment straight into their living rooms, or into the palm of their hand through a dozen different devices. People have invested in their homes, creating beautiful spaces for entertaining. During lockdown, industries related to home improvements thrived, as people invested in living spaces, including outdoor bars and entertaining areas that, in some cases, easily rival what the industry can offer because they're personalised.

At the same time, British supermarkets have increasingly used alcoholic products to drive footfall, making it harder for on-trade venues to compete. According to the Institute of Alcohol Studies, 'Supermarkets have frequently used alcohol as a loss leader to attract customers, selling it below cost price – a practice that has made it increasingly difficult for pubs, bars, and independent venues to compete on price.'[10]

When I first started, specialist alcohol could only be sourced from specialist suppliers. If you wanted a great wine list, you needed a great supplier, and those suppliers could secure better prices for us than our customers could obtain on their own. That's no longer the case. For many small venues, the best price available is on the supermarket shelf. I still remember my parents brewing homebrew because that was the only way to drink beer at home. Now, fantastic and exciting products are sold cheaply and easily, tucked next to the milk and cereals in the supermarket aisles. Hospitality businesses can no longer rely on being the place people go to access food and drink. That world has changed.

When we went out, we discovered new places almost by accident, often as 'passing trade'. We would walk past a place that looked nice, hear about it in the press, or go on recommendations from friends and family. Reaching customers back then felt more organic. Word of mouth was powerful. Press features and positive recommendations were gold dust. Today, communicating with customers and letting them know what you're about – what you have to offer – is harder. There's so much competing for attention.

Social media came along, opening up new opportunities. We could build online communities around our businesses, continue the conversation, and create a sense of FOMO. Now, it feels like too much. Too much information. Too many platforms. Too much noise. How do you stand out when the preferred way of getting attention is a space where you're not just competing with other local venues but against a global sea of content? A space where your customers are often more switched on, more knowledgeable, and moving faster than you can keep up with. It's overwhelming.

Then, you add the societal shifts over time. Everyone talks about how young people don't go out as much and drink less alcohol than previous generations. Research supports this: according to a 2021 report by Drinkaware, 21% of 18- to 24-year-olds in the UK identify as non-drinkers, compared with 13% of the overall adult population.[11] Young adults are choosing different ways to socialise, often centred less around alcohol and more around health, experience, and connection.

There is good news. Despite everything, spending on hospitality has remained strong. In fact, according to a 2024 report by Barclays, consumer spending on hospitality and leisure grew by 2.8% year-on-year – a sign that people still want, and need, to go out.[12] Other studies, including the Office for National Statistics' data, confirm that spending on restaurants and hotels remains robust, highlighting that people still value meaningful social experiences.[13]

While it may feel like customers are going out less and spending less, the reality is different. Customers today are more discerning. They're not necessarily spending less; they're making value decisions. When they go out, they're asking, 'Will this be worth it?' It's not just about how much money they have to spend; it's about whether the experience feels worth spending it on.

We're also seeing a shift in how they spend their money. Customers might be choosing fewer big-ticket experiences, but they're making up for it in smaller, everyday purchases. Quick treats, takeaway coffees, casual lunches – small decisions that still bring moments of joy and connection. When they do choose to go out for the bigger occasions, they care less about the cost because once they've decided it's worth it, they want to enjoy it fully.

The reality is that, after customers have chosen to go out, they're often less price-sensitive than we might think. The decision isn't just, 'How much have I got to spend?', but 'Is it worth going out at all?' If the answer is yes, then (within reason) the amount they spend matters less. Because when it's worth going out, they want it to be worth it properly.

It's made them more selective. They've become more mercenary. Customers will visit, appear to like you, and then never return. They're bolder too, more willing to tell you exactly what they think, what they like, and what they don't. They're more demanding and willing to point out mistakes, not just by voting with their feet, but by posting a review or telling you directly.

It might not sound like it, but this is a huge opportunity. Our customers know what they're looking for. Imagine that instead of taking your chances in all that noise and overwhelm, you become a beacon drawing in committed and loyal customers. Imagine that instead of trawling through dozens of venues and experiencing disappointment, they find you. You exceed their needs so fully that they never want to take the risk of going anywhere else. They stop searching.

Customers today are seeking places where they belong. Places where others like them gather. Places where they can bring their tribe – family, friends, colleagues – and meet new people, too. Places where they can sit in silence and still feel part of something, where they feel seen, valued, and their presence makes a difference.

This is what thriving hospitality businesses do. They stand out by becoming the place their customers are searching for, not by chasing every trend or trying to shout the loudest. They can tune out the noise, focus on what really matters, and build businesses that shine.

## How to win customers back

There's a clear pattern behind the businesses that do well. No matter the size, style, or location, the strongest businesses consistently focus on five things, which I call the Five Pillars of Stand Out Hospitality:

1. **Set High Standards:** Lead with consistency, clarity, and care.

2. **Stand Out:** Tune out the noise. Own your niche. Be unforgettable to the right people.

3. **Define Your Identity:** Be purpose driven. Know who you are and whom you serve.

4. **Build Belonging:** Create strong emotional connections with your customers and team.

5. **Tell A Great Story:** Share your 'why'. Let people in. Use storytelling to build visibility, trust, and loyalty.

In Part Two, we'll explore each of these pillars and how you can use them to create a business that feels good to run, stands out for the right reasons, and draws the right customers to you.

## Summary

This chapter highlights the reality that many of us already know: hospitality can be brutal. External shocks, rising costs, unpredictable weather, and shifting legislation all hit us the hardest. But when we asked operators to name the biggest issues they face, a pattern emerged. The challenges fall into three main areas: customers, teams, and overwhelm.

In this chapter, we took a closer look at customers. While people still want to go out, getting them through the door and keeping them feels harder than ever. There's more competition, noise, and reasons to stay home. Today's customers are more selective, demanding, and vocal. They're making decisions

## CORE CHALLENGES AND CUSTOMERS

based not just on price, but on value, asking themselves, 'Is this worth it?'

That shift might feel tough, but it's also your chance to stand out. If you can build something that feels right – something real, thoughtful, and emotionally on point – they'll find you. When they do, they'll stay loyal. Because what people are really looking for isn't just food and drink. It's connection. It's belonging.

## THREE
# The Team That Holds It All Together

The next theme that came up repeatedly in the ninety-nine problems survey was challenges related to the team.

Teams are more despondent and harder to engage. They're harder to recruit. They'll attend training and be enthusiastic for a while, but standards slip quickly. They're paid well; rewards are in place, and high-performance culture is there. On the surface, they may seem engaged and even bonded as a team, but behind the scenes lies constant effort: mentoring, coaching, nudging standards back up. They need more attention than ever. Even the most generous employers find themselves playing the role of in-house psychologists, and this level of personal attention is simply expected.

When things go wrong, everything is on a knife-edge. While a team may feel solid one day, the slightest disruption can cause it to fall apart. One person feeling below par due to a personal issue, a personality clash, or a source of tension is all it takes to throw the balance off completely, and discontent spreads quickly.

Leading and managing a team is, by far, the most challenging part of the work. Once I realised how important this part was, I knew my biggest responsibility was the team's coherence and happiness. Because if that broke down, how could we possibly deliver the standards our customers deserved?

I see the business as a set of concentric circles, like those created by dropping a pebble into a pond. I am the pebble. If I look after the team, they'll look after the customers. If I get my part right, my passion, purpose, and energy will ripple outwards. The team will feel it. The customers will feel it. That's how word of mouth begins. But, like a game of Chinese whispers, clarity matters. My focus was always on the team, and on making sure they understood, felt involved, and cared as much as I did.

Training is the start. Not just technical training, but training in the 'why': customer service, values, purpose, and the reality of what this work demands. Hospitality isn't learned from a handbook. This industry teaches you on the job. Shoulder-to-shoulder mentoring is how people learn. That's why apprenticeships

## THE TEAM THAT HOLDS IT ALL TOGETHER

are so successful. Often, new staff are thrown in at the deep end and expected to figure it out. In other industries, that might be seen as negligent, but in hospitality, it's often the best way to learn. You learn and discover your priorities by asking questions, watching others, and being guided by those more experienced around you. That's how chefs learn. It's how bar staff learn. You learn to juggle all the information and make smart decisions for the customer, the team, and yourself.

Sorting a large amount of information, quickly and under pressure, is part of the job. Some pick it up naturally, while others have to learn it. I've seen people buckle under the pressure – not because they didn't care, but because the job never became the fun, fast challenge it's meant to be. It just made them miserable.

My background is front of house. I particularly loved the maître d' role, and knowing what was happening at every table at all times. Holding all that information in your head, sorting it into priorities, guiding the team, making sure every customer had a great experience – it was a joy. Managing the pass from front of house and acting as the bridge between the kitchen and the customer were equally rewarding. I enjoyed watching the timing, checking in with the team, and serving as a second pair of eyes on every dish.

In 2021, after lockdown, I opened a pub in the middle of an industry-wide staffing crisis and found myself stepping into the role of head chef. It was something I had promised myself I'd never do, but there I was, learning on the job. Trying to run the business from the back seat. It was difficult. I don't know whether it was my age and my brain not working as well as it used to, or if the job really is just that hard.

There has always been a quiet battle in hospitality as to which is tougher: front of house or kitchen. I've done both. I can say, hand on heart, they're both brutal in their own ways. Over time, I learned to love the rhythm of each. At the front of house, I lived in the flow of the room – the energy, awareness, and service choreography. In the kitchen, it was precision, pressure, and pace – symphony under fire. Different beats, same goal.

There were moments in the kitchen when I was ten tickets deep, dishes stacked high, running the pass solo, cooking, plating, hitting time targets, while someone popped in to ask where the ketchup was, that I felt like I was trying to complete a Sudoku, word search, Rubik's cube, and *The New York Times* crossword all at once… to a stopwatch, in perfect synchronisation.

Both are tough jobs. Mostly, you learn by doing. That's why clarity matters. When the pressure's high and people are learning on the job, you need someone steady at the centre; skill alone is not enough to hold everything together. You need someone who is not only coordinating tasks, but also offering focus, purpose, and direction. In this industry, people need more than training; they need to know where they fit, what matters most, and how to work together as one. Because, despite how different they seem, front of house and kitchen are both working towards the same goal: the customer experience. To deliver that well, teams need someone who helps them see the whole picture: what are we here for? What are we trying to achieve together?

The most effective operators I know don't hold back. They share openly. They bring people in. If you want to succeed, let your team in. Let them help. Is hospitality really harder now? When it comes to running a team, the answer is yes. Not because people don't care or aren't capable, but because the world of work has shifted. Expectations have evolved. What used to be enough – working harder, staying later, and leading by example alone – doesn't cut it any more.

## A new generation, a new standard

I'm firmly a Gen Xer. When I started in hospitality, a full-time week was at least sixty hours. Anything less and you were considered part-time. Without the minimum wage, you had to work those hours just to survive. My boyfriend and I were both in the industry – I was front of house; he was a chef – and we worked seventy- to eighty-hour weeks just to pay the bills. It was hard, but it wasn't seen as a hardship. We were young and in it together, full of energy and learning something new every day.

We all smoked, drank, and lived on caffeine. There was no such thing as alcohol-free days because, for us, work was the alcohol-free day. We started early, worked straight through without breaks, barely ate, and then gathered at the end of the night over a drink to share the stories, the chaos, the little wins. It was our world.

But it was never sustainable. Many people fell by the wayside. The environment was toxic. What we now recognise as bullying or exploitation was accepted. Everyone worked beyond their scheduled hours. We had chefs throwing pans, front-of-house staff in tears, and nobody really questioned it. Drug and alcohol abuse was rife. There were kitchen initiation rituals. 'Banter' was often sexist or foul. Women were driven out or shut down. If you couldn't keep up, you weren't tough enough. That was the narrative. Those of us who survived were considered hospitality heroes. Surviving the brutality of the system was our badge of honour.

When I started running my own venues, it mattered deeply to me that things were different. I wanted to treat people well. We created businesses that nurtured, cared, and gave support. Businesses that saw people as individuals. We challenged what had come before and tried to build something better.

## THE TEAM THAT HOLDS IT ALL TOGETHER

Decades later, the industry has come a long way. We know how toxic it can be if we don't challenge. We talk openly about mental health now. We recognise how much of the industry has encouraged alcohol, drug use, and unhealthy lifestyles. The burnout isn't just personal; it's structural. It was built into the system.

No wonder, when lockdown happened, so many people left. Suddenly, they had space to reflect. They realised other industries existed. Some roles required less skill and paid more, with greater flexibility. For many, lockdown was the break they didn't even know they needed, and they never came back. That's the problem. For many people, it still doesn't feel like hospitality is worth it. I spoke earlier in this book about what we love about the industry. Not everyone feels that. For every person who had an amazing first experience and fell in love, there must be at least three others who didn't, either because the environment wasn't right for them or because they ran into the negative side first.

In the Kith & Kin podcast, nearly every guest I speak with has had at least one bad experience. Sometimes it was a horrible boss. Sometimes they pushed themselves too hard. Sometimes there was no one to say it's OK to slow down. The pressure to perform was relentless. Burnout was everywhere. That's why Kris Hall's launch of The Burnt Chef Project in 2019 struck such a chord. Initially sparked by his own experiences and frustrations with the culture of silence around mental health in hospitality, the project set out to break the stigma, open up honest conversations, and provide real support for those struggling behind the scenes. It wasn't just chefs who got it; the whole industry did. The mental health toll was real, and someone finally said it out loud.

Since then, The Burnt Chef Project has grown into a global movement, with a following that spans the world and partnerships in over thirty countries. Its message has reached millions through social media, events, training programmes, and workplace support initiatives. What began as a single voice has become a trusted, visible force for change, showing that vulnerability is not weakness and that no one in hospitality should have to suffer alone.[14]

The world has changed. Millennials shifted the way we think about work, and Generation Z is running with it. I appeared on the Strive podcast – a twelve-week series exploring workplace culture and generational change – hosted by Linda Neville, founder of Strive Employee Wellbeing. In the episode on hospitality, we talked about how Generation Z is revolutionising workplace culture. In one stride, they're doing what it took Generation X decades to chip away at.[15]

Now, if a workplace is toxic, it's called out. Bullying carries consequences. Employers are responsible for protecting their teams. It's not OK for a chef to shout at a young server. Generation Z will tell you if they need support with neurodiversity. They'll be open about mental health. They'll tell you about personal issues going on outside of work, and they expect understanding. The power dynamic has shifted. They know the market is transient. They know their time has value. They won't tolerate environments that harm them. The law is on their side, and they know it. They're not scared of walking away.

Minimum wage increases mean our teams are paid fairly for the hours they work. It also means they don't need to work unsustainable hours to survive. We used to have the option to opt out of the forty-eight-hour workweek. That opt-out allowed employers to legally ask employees to work longer hours, but now, hardly anyone signs it. Post 2020, I didn't have a single team member sign one. We're moving closer to a forty-hour work week norm – and thank goodness. Our teams deserve a life outside of work, and they shouldn't be too exhausted to enjoy it.

But there's a knock-on effect. If our teams are working forty hours instead of eighty, we need twice as many people to cover the same ground. So, there's a staffing crisis. It's partly down to Brexit, lockdown, and reputation, but it's also just maths. We need more people. It's a huge challenge – even if it's the right one.

Generation Z is also teaching the rest of us to expect more. While it's a challenge for operators, it's also a huge step forwards. Long live the revolution.

As a Generation X mother of four Generation Z kids, I'm proud of the role we've played. We raised them to challenge systems, expect better, and walk away when they're not treated well. Well done to them. And well done to us. But it's not easy, not for employers or managers. We're now being asked to nurture every member of staff on an individual basis. There's no medal for the extra time or the extra cost. We don't earn loyalty by doing this; it's just another overhead.

Generation X gave everything and hoped someone would notice. We defined ourselves by our effort. Generation Z define themselves by meaning. They know their worth. They take a job because it suits them right now. They smile, do the training, and give their best, but it's a transaction. They're being paid. They don't necessarily see it as a career. They will do a great job while they're with you, but they're also looking for the role that truly means something to them. Stand-out hospitality businesses know how to tap into that. They know how to connect purpose and belonging. I'll explain later in the book just how simple that shift is and how it can powerfully engage your team, reduce turnover and training costs, and start saving you time and money from day one.

In the next chapter, let's take a look at the final challenge that came up in the ninety-nine problems survey: overwhelm.

## Summary

This chapter explored the second big challenge identified by the ninety-nine problems survey: the team. Even when you're doing everything right – paying well, offering training, and building a positive culture – something still feels off. Standards slip. Energy dips. You spend more time coaxing, explaining, and holding things together than running the business.

We explored what's going on. How one person can throw the whole thing off. How leadership now means being part manager, part mentor, and part therapist. How post-lockdown shifts, generational change, and new expectations have made it harder to hold your team together and even harder to keep them motivated.

We also saw the truth that's been there all along. Hospitality has always demanded clarity, rhythm, and steady hands at the centre. People learn best when they're brought in, shown the whole picture, and given something to care about.

Generation Z is asking for more, and they're right to. They're showing us what 'better' looks like. Not everyone wants a career in this industry, but when you build the right environment, those who do want to pursue it will thrive. The rest will still show up and give their best.

## FOUR
# Overwhelm: The Weight We Carry

I still remember how angry I felt after participating in a conversation during lockdown about how to support the industry as we came out of it. A well-meaning businessperson suggested that we needed to find a way to encourage CEOs to mentor and support independent business owners. I can still feel my blood boil thinking of it, because that suggestion carried the assumption that those of us who start businesses as independents are simply aspiring CEOs, and what's holding us back is a lack of knowledge, or worse, a faulty mindset. The reality is, CEOs don't do the same job as we do.

Most CEOs have risen through the corporate world, climbing the ladder through departments within large organisations – organisations that, regardless of their scale, have silos and support structures. They oversee and lead, but they're surrounded by experts across various departments, including R&D, design, HR, marketing, sales, customer services, finance, IT, procurement, and legal.

In an independent hospitality business, the managing director, owner, or leader *is* all of those departments. They have to be creative, doing branding, marketing, product development, and experience design. They must understand the legal side: HR, licensing, food safety, fire safety, and compliance. They run customer service from end to end; not only the process, but the execution. Holding the door open. Smiling. Seating guests. Explaining the menu. Taking feedback. Dealing with complaints. Issuing apologies. Acting as the PR department in a crisis.

They design all the systems. They are the IT department when something breaks. They negotiate with suppliers, do the books, and manage payroll. They handle rotas, disciplinaries, and internal communications. They train the team, mediate team disputes, offer a shoulder to cry on, deliver one-to-ones, and source external support.

They stay on top of industry news, government policy, and legislative changes. They read the accounts, pitch to funders, and present to stakeholders. They interview new hires and onboard them personally.

They carry a heavy set of keys and know exactly which key opens what. When the toilet floods or the vegetable order doesn't turn up, they clean the floor or run to the supermarket. They chop coriander, slice lemons, light fires, calm customers, mow the grass, book the PAT testing, test the fire alarms, check invoices, pay the bills, juggle the cash flow, make the beds, run the socials, write emails, book bands, and hold everything together.

So, when it comes to business knowledge, CEOs may be brilliant at what they do, but it's not the same. Their insights don't always translate. Running a marketing campaign when you have a graphics department and a communications team is one thing. Trying to fit marketing in between running service, calling in orders, and jumping on the pass is an entirely different world.

This work is overwhelming. Of course it is, given we're running incredibly complex operations, while short on time, people, money, and energy. It's an endless balancing act, and when one aspect tips off balance, we feel it as overwhelm. Left unchecked, overwhelm leads to burnout, illness, and exhaustion. We've all seen too many examples of that.

The real, everyday fear that so many of us carry is failure. We start full of hope. We're optimistic. We believe in the dream of building something special, doing something different, and living a life of freedom, creativity, and meaning. We know others have failed, but we believe we'll be the exception. I've been that person. Every time I opened a new business, I believed it would be easier than the last; that I had learned enough and had it sussed. No matter how much you know or how well you plan, there will be times when you feel overwhelmed. The danger is being unable to get that overwhelm under control, and it spilling over, because some things are simply outside your control.

## The cost of carrying it all

This industry has broken me. Physically. Financially. I've hit the floor. In the space of just twenty-four hours, I lost two businesses. That meant fifty staff made redundant, two companies were in liquidation, and months of mess ensued, as I tried to do the right thing as a director. It meant facing bankruptcy. Worst of all, I lost my home. The family home I shared with my husband and our four children.

I lived most people's worst fear. Beyond the financial fallout, it was the shame that hurt most. Within hours, the story was online. The local paper. Trolls. Judgement. People thought that I was the big bad boss who left people unpaid and out of work. You're in the worst place not to look, so you look. And it stings. It cuts.

What if everything goes wrong? What if I get it wrong? What if I can't recover? What if I have to admit to my partner, my family, and my team that I failed? These are the fears that so many hospitality owners carry with them every day.

None of this should stop you.

There's a quote from Theodore Roosevelt that I've often returned to. It's referred to as the 'Man in the Arena' speech.[16] He talks about how it's not the critic who counts, but rather the person who takes action. The credit belongs to the one who's actually in the arena, whose face is marred by dust, sweat, and blood. The one who may stumble but keeps trying again and again. The one who may fail but dares greatly. Even in failure, they have dared more than those who never even tried.

This idea matters to me. So much so that I have it pinned up by my front door and see it every time I leave the house. Even if I fail, even if I fall flat, I would rather get in the ring, show up, and give it everything. At least I know I lived it. That I was in the arena. That I tried.

Still, we need to be realistic about the risks. We need to face them instead of flinching away from them. We need to do what we can to mitigate them. The world is moving fast. Since 2020, we've seen a tidal wave of change – legislation, costs, and culture – and it's hard to keep up. Margins are tighter. Expectations are higher. Though we're a resilient, innovative, agile bunch, doing it all alone is harder than ever.

My risk appetite is high, and it's matched by my optimism and tenacity. That's not true for everyone, and that's OK. We all have our own approach. I'd rather be brave and risk falling than sit on the sidelines watching someone else do what I know I'm capable of. This isn't about judgement. We're not all meant to be the same. Extroverts may have evolved to be the first ones out of the cave, the first to the food and fun, thriving in the good times. But when the predators came, it was the introverts, tucked away, quiet and cautious, who survived.

We need a balance. We need each other. I bring energy, ideas, and a fair amount of chaos. Those who work with me know what I leave in my wake. That's why I surround myself with people who thrive on order. They might pretend to be appalled by the chaos, but secretly, they love using their spreadsheets to tidy up my mess! It's important to know your tolerance for risk. Know your limits regarding your time, energy, and relationships. Set bold goals, but be honest about what it might cost you.

Don't compare your journey to anyone else's. For example, the commonly bandied-about notion that successful people get up super early, do a heavy workout, and start their day while everyone else is still in bed is nonsense. It's a formula that might work for early risers, but most of us in hospitality are night owls. Five o'clock should only happen once a day. That doesn't make us less driven, capable, or committed; we're just wired differently. So, know yourself. Know your rhythms. Know when to stop. Success isn't about copying someone else's schedule. It's about building one that works for you.

The reality is we all hit a wall. In *The Dip*, Seth Godin describes that moment when things stop being exciting and get hard, and most people quit.[17] He calls it the dip. I call it the sticky bit. It's the point where things become boring, repetitive, lonely, and frustrating – it's exactly this point that matters most.

Starting something is thrilling. People cheer you on, and early wins get big applause. But no one talks about the messy middle, when the novelty wears off and the real work begins. This is the part that separates those who succeed from those who stop. It's not about perfection. It's about consistency. It's about choosing to keep going when things feel heavy. When the initial fire's gone. When it's hard. If you're still there, turning up and trying when it would be easier to quit, then you're exactly where you need to be.

That said, it's also OK to say enough if it's not right for you any more. Knowing when to let go is not a failure; it shows wisdom. Sometimes the bravest thing isn't pushing through but stepping back. I once closed a restaurant. In the press release announcing the closure, I said the area wasn't ready for us. The truth is I wasn't ready for it. It might have worked one day. We had national press coverage and rave reviews. It was the kind of stuff that feeds your ego, but it wasn't feeding us – it wasn't feeding the business. After two and a half years, I stopped pouring money into it. I needed to consolidate what I had left. I stood in front of my team with my two-week-old daughter in my arms and told them we were closing. It was brutal. There were tears. Because it mattered. Because they loved it, and it meant something. But I knew I didn't have the capacity to keep taking that level of risk.

Many of the most important lessons that I share in the rest of this book came from that moment. The moment I let go. The moment I learned the difference between businesses that survive and businesses that stand out.

## Seven common mistakes operators make (and what thriving businesses do instead)

Let's take a moment to pause. So far, we've explored why hospitality matters, why many of us are drawn to it, and where our deep sense of purpose comes from. We've also looked at the three core challenges facing hospitality leaders today. With that context in mind, it's the perfect time to talk about something just as important: what *not* to do when things get tough.

I'll say it again: hospitality has always been in crisis. We live on the front line of constant change. When the weather shifts, we see it reflected in bookings. When a government minister opens their mouth, it changes our weekend. When the economy dips, we don't simply read about it in the headlines; we live it minute by minute. That's what makes hospitality both exhilarating and exhausting.

Operators in this industry are brilliant. We're creative, resilient, entrepreneurial problem-solvers. We rise to the challenge because we care. We want to make something meaningful. We want to serve. But when that energy starts to run low, when the endless waves of uncertainty keep hitting, it's easy to slip into survival mode. That's when we start reaching for short-term fixes.

Before we dive into the solutions, let's talk about the traps. There are seven common mistakes that independent hospitality business owners make when things get hard:

1. Doing more instead of doing differently

2. Overtraining instead of leading

3. Overinvesting in systems instead of shaping culture

4. Chasing short-term marketing fixes

5. Following the competition instead of defining your own path

6. Discounting instead of creating value

7. Looking for quick fixes instead of facing the truth

These aren't criticisms; they're patterns – behaviours I've seen again and again, not only in others but in myself. When times are tough, it's natural to default to what feels safe, seems productive, or has worked before. Sometimes, those instincts can keep us stuck. Here's a fresh look at the most common mistakes and what stand-out hospitality businesses do instead.

## 1. Doing more instead of doing differently

When bookings slow or the team is short-staffed, it's instinctive to step in. We pull extra shifts, redo the rota, and patch the holes. We roll up our sleeves because we care. It feels honourable. It feels familiar. But over time, it becomes a trap.

The more time you spend inside the business, the less time you have to lead it. You lose sight of the patterns, the possibilities, the warning signs. You become essential to the day-to-day, but absent from the direction.

What stand-out operators do instead: step back to step up. They protect space for strategy. They build a team that can function without them. Not because they're lazy, but because they know leadership requires perspective.

## 2. Overtraining instead of leading

We care about standards. We care about our team. So, when something slips, we reach for training. More sessions. More manuals. More repetition. Often, the team already knows what to do. The issue isn't knowledge; it's consistency, clarity, and care.

Stand-out businesses lead by example. They don't just train – they live their standards. They set the tone daily. They have strong internal cultures that make great behaviour the default. Training supports the culture but doesn't replace it.

### 3. Overinvesting in systems instead of shaping culture

Systems are important. Training manuals and processes have their place. But culture is what your team actually absorbs. It's what they follow. You can write down the perfect way to clean a barista station, but if the culture says 'rush it', that's what will happen. People tend to emulate those around them. That's human nature.

Stand-out businesses build systems, but they also shape behaviour. They define and defend their culture. They embody it.

### 4. Chasing short-term marketing fixes

When the numbers dip, panic marketing kicks in. Discounts, last-minute posts, ads, campaigns – we try to do everything, everywhere, all at once. Without a clear message, it's all just noise. And customers can feel it.

Stand-out operators market with purpose. They know their brand and their people. They show up consistently, not frantically. Their message is steady, and it resonates.

## 5. Following the competition instead of defining your own path

It's so tempting to look sideways. To see what others are doing and assume you should do it too. But you never know the full story. The competition might have a different model, audience, or agenda. What seems successful might be costing them more than it's bringing in.

Stand-out businesses tune out the noise. They listen inwardly to their customers, their values, and their vision. They build something that's right for them. Something worth following, not copying.

## 6. Discounting instead of creating value

Lowering prices can feel like the only option. It's reactive and immediate. You hope it keeps people coming. But it's rarely sustainable, and it undermines your worth.

Stand-out businesses focus on value. They elevate the experience. They create connection, trust, and meaning. When people feel something, they come back, and price becomes less relevant.

## 7. Looking for quick fixes instead of facing the truth

In the toughest moments, it's natural to look for a lifeline: a course, guru, or silver bullet that will make it all click into place. But there is no magic fix. The hardest truth is also the most freeing: you already know more than you think.

Stand-out operators stop searching for perfect answers and start doing honest work. They reflect. They seek community. They clarify what matters and build from there.

Highlighting these seven common mistakes isn't about judging; it's about recognition. We've all slipped into these patterns, especially when things get tough. The shift begins when we start to notice what's no longer working and choose something better. Sustainable businesses don't just survive, they get clarity. They lead with consistency. They stop doing more and start doing differently. They build businesses that stand out because they stand for something. They create emotional connections, not just transactions. They tell stories that people remember.

That's what this book is here to help you do. So, let's begin with the work that matters most. If the mistakes are symptoms, then the real solutions start at the root: how you lead. At the centre of every thriving hospitality business is a leader who represents the standard to uphold. A leader who knows what matters and shows up for their team and customers with clarity, care, and consistency.

That's where we start. If you want to change your results, you have to raise the bar, starting with yourself.

## Summary

This chapter took a hard look at the emotional and practical weight that independent operators carry every day. This isn't the same job as a CEO. We don't just oversee – we do it all. From branding and compliance to chopping lemons and unblocking toilets, we're the ones with the keys, the answers, the vision, and the risk.

You heard the reality behind the overwhelm, and what it means to carry a business on your shoulders. You saw what happens when that weight tips: burnout, shame, and fear of failure. You also saw what sets us apart: the courage to keep going. The grit to get back up. The heart to continue caring, even when things go wrong.

We named the pressures and the patterns: the seven most common mistakes good operators make when things get hard. Not in criticism, but in recognition, because we've all been there. The fix isn't about doing more; it's about doing differently. That starts with gaining clarity, raising your standards, and building something you believe in, even when the pressure is high.

---

### QUESTIONS TO CONSIDER:
**Seven common mistakes**

This chapter wasn't about blame; it was about awareness. Once you recognise the patterns, you can choose differently. So, take a breath and get honest.

- Which of these seven mistakes have you fallen into recently?
- Where are you over-functioning instead of stepping back?
- Where are you following noise not clarity?
- Where are you waiting for a fix, instead of trusting yourself to lead?

Now, the shift:

- What would change if you stopped trying to do more and started doing things differently?
- What's one way you can lead, rather than chase, this week?
- What decision have you been postponing that's really about courage, not capacity?

This isn't about doing everything at once. It's about choosing one thing you'll no longer tolerate – and one new standard you'll lead with.

---

# PART TWO
## THE FIVE PILLARS: A FRAMEWORK FOR STAND OUT HOSPITALITY

## FIVE
# Set High Standards

Before we talk about standards for others, let's start with those you set for yourself. Before thinking about your team, customers, or even strategy, you need to come back to yourself. Your business doesn't sit outside of you; it is built around you. You are not separate from it. You set the tone.

Before you even begin to build using the Five Pillars, ask yourself the questions that really matter: why do you do what you do? What lifestyle are you trying to create? What makes you happy? How much discomfort can you tolerate? How long can you keep going when it's hard (because it will be hard)?

Think of your business as concentric circles. At the centre is you, the pebble. Everything else – your team, culture, and customer experience – ripples out from you. If the centre isn't strong, nothing else can hold. Before you can look after anyone else, you have to look after yourself. Before you reward others, you need to reward yourself, emotionally and practically.

If you haven't done this thinking and aren't anchored in your own reasons for what you do, it's too easy to lose your way when things get tough. You start chasing shiny new fixes. You build a business that looks good but no longer feels like yours. As Simon Sinek, author of *Start With Why* and a global thought leader on purpose-driven leadership, said: 'People don't buy what you do; they buy why you do it.'[18] If you don't know what that is or you lose sight of it, it shows in your decisions, presence, and the energy you bring to the work.

You know why you started. You know your passion and excitement. You know why this industry meant something to you. But it's worth writing it down. What do you love? What don't you enjoy? What lights you up? What drains you? Once you're clear on what you need and what it's all for, everything else becomes simpler. Decision-making sharpens. You show up differently. The business you build will feel like home. Before you can lead others, you have to lead yourself.

If you're in a partnership or working with funders, that clarity is even more vital. You don't have to be driven by the same thing as them, but you do need to be honest with each other. The kind of honesty that's sometimes uncomfortable. I've had partnerships that created something extraordinary, and one that failed. That failure took the whole business with it. We thought we were aligned, but we hadn't made our expectations clear. I was building something that excited me, assuming it would work for both of us, but I missed something he needed. And he wasn't honest about his limits or how much he could give. We hadn't done the work.

## The invisible weight we carry

You've built something personal; now you have to protect it. That's what leadership really is. It's not just about setting goals, running day-to-day operations, or coming up with new ideas. It's holding space and carrying the emotional load that allows everything else to function.

When we set high standards in hospitality, it can be easy to fall into the trap of thinking they're just about performance. Rules. Expectations. Outcomes. Really, they're about people. They're about building an environment where others can thrive and doing so with compassion.

The truth is that leadership in hospitality is lonely work. You are the one who needs to show up every day and keep it all together. Your customers expect consistency. They want to see your smiling face, share in your enthusiasm, and be hosted with energy and ease. They expect that – always. Your job is to make people feel special. To offer them an escape, a safe space, a sense of belonging. Even when you've had no sleep, you're worried about finances, or everything behind the scenes is falling apart.

Even when you've built real friendships with customers, there's still a gap. They might share their darkest moments with you, but it's necessary in your role that you shield them from yours. The unspoken truth of service is that we put others first. In doing so, we often stand slightly apart.

I joke with other operators about team WhatsApp groups: every business has one group for everyone and another for everyone except the boss. It's funny, but it's also real. That slight separation is part of leadership. Your team might love working with you, but they still look to you to hold it together and know what's next (even when you don't).

This weight is invisible, but it's heavy. I see it every day in the owners and leaders I work with. They lead with heart. They care deeply about their people. They see potential where others see problems. They coach, support, mediate, and mentor. They carry the emotional load, always looking out for others and steadying the ship. They do it quietly, consistently, and with love. It's a huge part of what makes hospitality such a

## SET HIGH STANDARDS

powerful and human industry. It's also why burnout is so common.

No matter how generous or compassionate you are, leadership demands hard decisions. And that can be incredibly lonely. The hardest decisions aren't operational; they're personal. Like realising someone on your team isn't right for the role, even though you like them. Or choosing between protecting your team and keeping a loyal customer happy. Or doing what's right for the business, knowing someone might dislike you for it.

Sometimes, it's not even about a mistake; it's about misalignment. Take the woman I hired, whose energy was boundless. She was warm, open, and deeply enthusiastic, lifting everyone's spirits. But in my quiet, private members' club, her style didn't fit. Her approach wasn't wrong; she just needed a different kind of stage.

That's leadership, too: knowing when the fit isn't right, even though it breaks your heart. Not everyone is meant to belong. They're simply not right for your business. Even the most inclusive, purpose-led brands aren't for everyone, and your venue is no different. Sometimes a bad review isn't about a bad experience. It's just a mismatch. The customer came to the wrong place. The same goes for your team.

How do we lead through these moments with strength and compassion? When someone isn't meeting expectations (for example, lateness becomes a pattern or something feels off), it's important to start from a place of understanding, not judgment. Ask yourself three questions:

1. Is this a leadership issue? Have I been clear about my expectations, communicated well, and modelled consistently?

2. Is there a skills gap? Do they know how to do what I'm asking? Am I assuming knowledge they haven't had a chance to learn?

3. Is this a life situation? Is something else going on? Is this a time to listen, offer flexibility, or show care?

Compassionate leadership doesn't mean lowering the bar. It means facing things head-on, with honesty and empathy. Sometimes, we support someone to grow. Sometimes, we let them go. Either way, we lead with integrity.

When we avoid the hard conversations, we don't protect people – we avoid taking responsibility. And that responsibility is real. Even when you have mentors, coaches, or supportive partners, it's still you who has to make the call most of the time. That's what you signed up for. That doesn't mean it's easy.

Susan Scott, author of *Fierce Conversations*, shares her philosophy that the conversation is the relationship. If you're not having the right conversations, your business will suffer. There's a quote from her that's stayed with me: 'Never be afraid of the conversations you are having. Be afraid of the conversations you are not having.'[19] That line changed how I lead. Avoiding discomfort doesn't protect your team; it weakens your business. It chips away at trust. It sets the wrong tone.

Throughout my career, I've faced many difficult situations. I've had to let go of team members like the woman whose sharp intelligence entertained me but whose inconsistency affected everyone. I've dealt with a young man who thought leadership meant confrontation. In those early years, I watched the kitchen staff 'tease' the waitresses and didn't speak up. I told myself I was being kind, but I wasn't setting the standard.

Now I know better. Standards protect the team. Silence, especially from the leader, is dangerous. Leadership means stepping into discomfort. Having the conversations no one else wants to have. Doing the things others won't. Protecting your people, your standards, and your business. You hold the line. Even when it's lonely, even when no one sees it, you're the reason the whole thing stays standing.

## Pride, not perfection

Setting high standards isn't about control or micromanagement; it's about pride. Not the showy kind, but the kind that lives quietly in the details. The kind that guides how you set a table, clear a glass, train your team, or check the lights before you lock up. That's where excellence starts.

Marketing thinker Seth Godin once said: 'You don't have to be perfect. But you do have to be prepared to be the best in the world.'[20] It's from *The Practice*, a book about creative work that's generous, intentional, and consistent. And he's right – it's not about ego. It's about commitment and choosing to show up with care. Not to be flawless, but to matter.

And no, 'best in the world' doesn't mean Michelin stars. It means being the best in your customer's world, in that moment, on that visit. Making the coffee that hit the spot or giving them the welcome they didn't know they needed. Every visit is a treat. They didn't have to walk through your door. They could have boiled the kettle, cracked open a tin, or swung by the supermarket. But they came to you. They chose to spend their money, time, and energy in your space. That's a privilege.

Yet we forget. We treat hospitality like a transaction, as though food and drink are the only things that matter. That's when standards slip. Not because we don't care, but because we forget that customers do. Then customers stop coming back, not because they didn't like the food, but because they didn't feel seen.

## SET HIGH STANDARDS

You know the feeling. You walk into a venue and sense the indifference. Staff finish their conversation before acknowledging you. You're handed something without eye contact or warmth. Payment is requested before you've even been recognised as a person. It's demoralising. It turns what could have been a human moment into just another errand.

That's not why people come.

The product matters, but it's only part of the picture. The rest is the feeling. The connection. The sense that someone noticed, welcomed, and remembered you. That you mattered. If your team sees customers as just another task – another box to tick – then you've missed the point, because every visit is a special occasion for someone. They might be celebrating. Escaping. Mourning. Starting over. Meeting someone new. Or just needing a moment. You may not always know the reason, but that doesn't make it less important. If all you offer is a transaction, why would they come back? They can get that anywhere.

Customers can tell when a business upholds high standards. They feel it in the warmth of the welcome, how a table is cleared, in the act of holding the door open for them, and in the cleanliness of the toilets. (Because if those are neglected, what does it say about kitchen hygiene? Training? Leadership?) Everything is connected.

This is where consistency comes in. Not perfection, but reliability. Your team needs to know what's expected of them, and they need to see you model it. If you're inconsistent, distracted, or always changing your mind, they won't trust you. If they don't trust you, they won't follow. Lead with pride. Show them what excellence looks like. Be the person who notices the fallen cushion, the dusty skirting board, the plate that isn't hot enough. Because excellence is a choice you make every day, not just when it's easy.

Your business isn't merely a venue; it's someone's moment. That moment deserves your best. If you want your standards to last, they need to be deeply rooted.

## Protect what matters

We are here to serve. That's the heart of it. We don't do this work to chase stars or collect likes. We do it to create something meaningful for our customers, our team, and ourselves. But when the days grow long and comparison creeps in, it's easy to forget that and start measuring your worth by someone else's version of success. It's tempting to think the next five-star review or award will finally prove you're good enough. If we're not careful, we can start building our businesses for the wrong reasons and the wrong people. We can start making decisions based on fear, ego, or the need to be seen. Slowly, we can lose sight of what we're really here for.

## SET HIGH STANDARDS

So, take a moment and honestly ask yourself: who are you doing this for?

Because when you're truly proud of what you've built – when it reflects your values, your care, and your intention – your team and customers can feel it. That kind of pride lifts the energy of the room. It creates a culture where people want to show up and give their best. But if you're doing it for the applause, that feeling fades. The buzz dies down. The pressure resets. And you'll find yourself back where you started, unsure of who you're trying to please.

Let's be clear: there's nothing wrong with wanting good reviews or the occasional award. They matter. They can be useful tools for visibility, trust, and credibility. But that's what they are – tools, not strategy. They should support your purpose, not replace it. When they are a by-product of great work, they're gold. But if they become the goal, you'll always be chasing.

Danny Meyer, author of *Setting the Table* and one of the most respected voices in modern hospitality, believes hospitality is a dialogue, not a monologue. It's not about showing off or impressing people into silence; it's about presence.[21] Listening. Making people feel truly seen and cared for.

So take pride in what you've built – not because others say it's good, but because you know it is. Because it holds up. Because it feels right. Set your standard. Define your version of success. Stand by the quality of what you deliver and the impact it has on the people you serve. If you don't feel proud of what you've built, that's the signal to realign yourself with what matters. That's where the work begins again.

Pride isn't arrogance; it's alignment. It's knowing your business reflects your values and vision. That's what makes it resilient. That's what allows it to stand tall, even when things get tough. Integrity doesn't need to shout loudly. It shows in the quiet details, such as the way your team speaks to guests and how your venue feels on a rainy Tuesday or a packed Saturday night. It shows in the things you don't let slide, and the things you protect at all costs.

When you lead with integrity, your business becomes something people trust. Something they feel part of. Something that matters. When that happens, as you'll see in the chapters to come, you don't need to chase loyalty because people will bring others to you.

## Surround yourself with excellence

If you want to raise your standards, start by improving your environment. Because your energy, ambition, and clarity are shaped by the people around you. You don't grow in a vacuum; you grow in community.

## SET HIGH STANDARDS

Jim Rohn, one of the original voices in personal development, put it simply: 'You are the average of the five people you spend the most time with.'[22] It's been quoted endlessly for a reason – it's true. When you're around people who hold themselves to high standards, take pride in their work, dream boldly, and act with intention, it rubs off. Excellence becomes normal. Expected.

That's exactly why I created Kith & Kin. Not from a strategy deck but from instinct. A gut feeling that we needed more connection, honesty, and shared learning. It began with people I respected – those who lifted me up, challenged me, and made me want to be better. That instinct has been there from the start.

When I opened my first venue, I'd spent years walking into places that came close to, but never quite matched, what I imagined. I knew something more was possible – something more thoughtful, more alive. I soaked up what others did well and quietly vowed to do better where they fell short. We're all magpies, really. Hospitality nerds notice everything. Sound levels. Menu copy. How the light falls across the bar. And yes, we take pictures of brilliant loos. We're always learning, always shaping what comes next. When we're around others who do the same, we become sharper. We grow. And we feel less alone.

This instinct to learn socially is part of what makes us human. In *Humankind: A hopeful history*, historian

Rutger Bregman notes that while Neanderthals had bigger brains and stronger bodies, they were individualistic. *Homo sapiens* shared knowledge and adapted faster. That's what helped them thrive.[23]

It's still true now. When you feel envy and catch yourself thinking, 'I wish I could do that', don't shrink from it. That's not weakness; it's your ambition talking. Let it guide you. Ask: what do I admire? What can I learn?

We're wired to grow within a community. The fastest way to elevate your leadership, standards, and entire business is to surround yourself with people who are already playing at the level you want to reach. Seek them out. Choose your circle with care. Let your environment raise the bar.

When you spend time with people who expect more, not only from others, but from themselves, you start to expect more, too. In turn, when your bar is raised, so is theirs. That's the kind of leadership that changes everything.

So, how do you uphold that standard and still carve your own path? How do you stay focused when the world keeps shouting louder?

Next, we explore how to stand out by tuning out the noise.

## Summary

True standards begin with you. In hospitality, consistency, clarity, and care aren't just things we expect from others; they're choices we model every day. This chapter explored what it means to lead with integrity. To set the tone from the inside out, hold steady through discomfort, and protect what matters most. It's not about control; it's about pride – the quiet kind that shows up in the details.

You are the first pebble in the ripple. Before you expect excellence from your team or consistency from your customers, you have to show up for yourself with honesty, courage, and care. When you lead from alignment, that energy flows outwards. Your standards set the tone, shape the culture, and create the conditions for trust, growth, and belonging.

It's not something you do alone. Surrounding yourself with excellence – peers, mentors, and team members who lift the bar – helps keep your values visible and your energy high. Set your standard, stand by it, and let everything ripple out from there.

---

**QUESTIONS TO CONSIDER:**
**Set high standards**

Lead with excellence. Uphold strong standards. Deliver consistent, high-quality experiences.

- Where in your business do your current standards fall short of what you expect?
- Are you leading in a way that encourages your team to follow and modelling the behaviour you expect from others?
- Where do you rely on personal effort or firefighting, rather than building systems and standards others can follow?
- What does consistency mean to you, and where could you be more consistent in delivery, leadership, or communication?
- What's one high standard you're proud of, and how can you protect or improve it?

# SIX
# Stand Out

As we discussed, when you set up and open your first place, you're usually driven by something more profound than simply wanting to run a business. There's a fire in your belly. A belief that you can do something special, that you can do things better. Sometimes it starts with a boss who didn't see your value. Sometimes it's sparked by a late-night chat with someone who shares your enthusiasm – someone who says, 'This is going to be the best place in the world.' You believe them. You believe in yourself. You're going to stand out. You're going to change the world.

That kind of energy can get you far. Add a generous dollop of optimism – the kind every great founder has – and you can charge in, full of purpose and drive, ready for whatever comes.

## When the noise takes over

The reality of hospitality is that, even if you take over an existing venue, those who have never done it before will look at your business and see something simple. One of our superpowers is paddling furiously beneath the surface while gliding on top, making it all look effortless. The customer sees the food, the drink, the smile, the experience; they don't see the chaos, the decisions, the trade-offs. How hard can it be? Pour a drink. Serve a dish. Post something decent on social media. Book a quiz night. Do a rota. Keep the books.

Since it looks simple, everyone has an opinion. Customers. Staff. Friends. Family. Suppliers. The general public. 'What you should do is...' becomes a daily refrain. After all, they eat out. They've stayed in hotels. They've seen what others are doing online. So, they must know, right?

I'm not saying don't listen to feedback – being open to ideas and different perspectives is vital. But being a hospitality operator means facing a lot of noise, and most of it isn't helpful. Most of it isn't rooted in your context, priorities, or purpose.

## The risk of becoming 'just another'

If you don't find a way to tune out that noise, you'll start drifting. You'll begin looking sideways. You'll notice what the coffee shop down the road is doing. You'll compare your prices with those of the chain next door. You'll see what's trending and feel like you're falling behind. You'll start wondering whether you should change your menu, your vibe, or yourself. Slowly, one well-meaning comment at a time will chip away at your identity.

Here's what happens when you try to appeal to everyone: you become nice. No one falls in love with nice. You become familiar, but not memorable. You become a place to eat or sleep, but not *their* place. If you want to build a business that truly lasts – one that customers love, remember, and return to – then you have to be brave enough to stand for something. To do that, you have to stop listening to the outside noise.

## The room of ten

Imagine walking into a room of ten people. You want them all to like you, so you moderate your behaviour. Perhaps only a little at first – soften a few opinions, tone down the parts that might be too much. You laugh in the right places, nod along, and work hard to be agreeable. They think you're nice, polite, pleasant. But the conversation moves around you. People are not that interested. You're there, but not really present. You leave the room feeling accepted, but not remembered.

Now imagine walking into the same room and being fully yourself. You're clear and honest. You don't perform, pretend, or hold back. A couple of people don't get you. A few decide you're not for them. Maybe you only really connect with two of the ten people. But those two? They stay and listen; they feel something resonate. You are at the centre of the conversation, not because you're trying to be, but because you're saying something that matters. You've sparked something real. That's the power of being true to who you are.

When you compromise too much and continually adjust your behaviour to please others, you chip away at yourself. Bit by bit, you lose clarity and energy. You become less certain and compelling. Eventually, you don't even recognise yourself. This isn't just about you; it applies to your business, too. You are not meant to be liked by everyone. Being nice is not the objective. If you want a stand-out business, you've got to be loved. That means knowing exactly who you are and having the courage to stay true to it. When you compromise, you don't just lose your edge; you lose connection. You end up being liked by everyone and loved by no one. When you lead with who you really are, you build something stronger, sharper, and stickier.

The global population is currently around 8.2 billion.[24] You and your business are not meant to be for all, so don't try to design it to suit everyone. Find your niche – the people who align with what you want and need from your business. Those who share your values and feel like part of your tribe. When your business reflects what you truly believe in, everything feels more aligned, more grounded, more 'you'. It becomes easier to make decisions, say no, and build something that people genuinely connect with.

## Say no to the noise

In the past, I've been guilty of not taking my own advice. In fact, it might be the hardest lesson for any operator to learn. When I took on an existing business, I felt a responsibility to maintain continuity, honour its history, and respect the voices of those who had known it before me. I thought I should stand back and listen. I felt I owed it to the people to take their opinions on board. Especially in pubs, there's a deeply embedded idea of what a pub should be – what and whom it should serve.

The sheer quantity of products alone was overwhelming: cask ales, lagers, draught ciders, a fridge full of bottled drinks, bar snacks, and menus featuring fish and chips, steaks, lunchtime cobs, and kids' pizzas. Then there were the events – the quizzes, bands, and Sunday roasts. I tried to do it all, and I became exhausted.

I had been wrong. What I needed to do was stand out, and I couldn't do that while I was chasing every other pub within a ten-mile radius, and there were many, all serving the same food and drinks at the same prices, and running the same events. Yes, I had a brilliantly trained team, and they were amazing, but the only thing I could compete on was great customer service and personality. While that might have cut it in the past, these days it isn't enough.

We became just another pub. With nothing unique to say, I had no way of being heard among the noise of social media. I had no way to grab the attention or imagination of the people I wanted to serve. I strayed too far from my own purpose and from the real needs of my customers. To succeed, I needed to define what I was going to say no to before even figuring out what to say yes to.

How do you know what to say no to? Two venues might look the same from the outside, but they can be wildly different. From the owner to the customer, there are thousands of variations in budget, energy, and the soul behind them. So, when a small coffee shop compares itself to a multinational like Starbucks or Costa, it doesn't make sense. To a passing customer, you might look like competitors, but you're playing a completely different game. You don't have their scale. You can't operate on their margins, and you certainly don't have the buying power to negotiate like they do.

## Strategic clarity over mass appeal

My city centre bar was small and had local, independent suppliers. For a venue of our size, our sales were strong. That made us popular with suppliers, who wanted to look after us. This was back when drinks companies really did spoil you. I've been to Germany on a beer tour. I was given tickets to everything: cricket, rugby, horse racing. Once, I even had a trip to Finland to see Father Christmas.

We could negotiate, but only up to a point. There was always a floor. A level below which suppliers wouldn't go, and rightly so. They were building businesses too, and supporting their own ecosystem. That's when I first realised: we weren't competing on volume. We didn't need to. On the rare occasion that a customer commented on our prices – perhaps comparing us to Wetherspoons – the explanation was easy. Wetherspoons operates at scale. They can buy cheap because they buy big. There were times when a pint in Wetherspoons cost less than I could buy it wholesale. That's the power of mass purchasing. I once saw Guinness pull out of Wetherspoons because they refused to discount further, arguing it would devalue the brand. Wetherspoons removed every Guinness tap from all their sites. The next day, Guinness gave in. That's scale in action.

That's not our world. Independents aren't playing that game, and we don't have to. Our value doesn't lie in shaving pennies off the bill. It lies in offering something people can't get anywhere else. So, when someone tells you what your prices should be – or you catch yourself comparing what you do to someone else – remember that context is everything. Scale is not your strategy; clarity is.

Every business is different, with its own structure, goals, strategy, and soul. Know what makes you different and lead with it. Let that difference be your strength. Niching is about clarity and bravery. It's about choosing a specific market segment, customer type, or experience that you can uniquely serve better than anyone else. Niching isn't about limiting yourself; it's about focusing your efforts, marketing, and identity to become unforgettable to your ideal customer. It gives you permission to say no to distractions and to double down on your strengths. When you choose a clear niche, you stop competing on price or convenience and instead compete on the depth of the experience you offer and the strength of your connection.

That burger that's half the price of yours? Maybe it's made with lower-quality ingredients. Perhaps it's aimed at a different market. Maybe it's sold at a loss to encourage people through the door. It doesn't mean you're doing it wrong. Just because it looks the same doesn't mean it is the same. So, be different. Stand out.

Begin here: what do you want from your business? Why does it matter to you? What do your customers want from your business? Why does it matter to them? When your purpose and theirs align, that's when the magic happens. You build your business around your strengths, what you care about, what you need, and the kind of life you want to live. I've done this myself with all of my businesses.

In my first business, I was twenty-three, child-free, and full of energy. I did everything: opened up, turned on the coffee machine, bottled up, greeted every customer, cashed up at the end of the night, and cleaned the toilets before I went home. And I loved it. That business was a reflection of who I was then – ambitious, hands-on, full-throttle.

Ten years later, it was a different story. I had four young children, three of whom are neurodivergent. I was burned out and couldn't work the long hours any more. My strengths had shifted. I was still a leader and a creator, but I needed more flexibility. I wanted to build something that could thrive even when I wasn't on the floor every day. So, I designed the business differently. I hired an exceptional general manager. I concentrated on recruitment, team culture, strategy, marketing, reputation, and the brand. I focused on the things only I could handle and gave myself permission to build the business around the life I needed.

Both businesses were successful. Customers who followed me from one to the other could feel the same thread – my values, the culture, the way we did things – running through, even though they were designed for completely different versions of me. That's the point. Your business doesn't have to look like anyone else's. It needs to reflect who you are and what you believe in.

## Even I've been *that* customer

Even so, sometimes I find myself being *that* customer – the know-it-all who thinks they have the answer. The one who can't help but offer a suggestion, even when the place is already doing exactly what it's meant to. I hate catching myself doing it, but it has happened.

There's a café I absolutely love. It's quirky, original, and has built a loyal following of people seeking an indulgent, joyful treat. They serve some of the best coffee I've ever tasted, in this old warehouse-style venue tucked away at the back of an industrial estate. You have to know it's there. It's strung with fairy lights, decorated with hand-drawn illustrations, and quirky stickers. It's a brilliant example of a business serving its tribe. Everyone who goes there knows they're part of something. They speak the same language. They share the same worldview, sense of taste, and a knowing smile with the staff and each other.

The business, Bitsy's Emporium of Awesome (even the name brings a smile), is owned by Charlotte, a master baker, whose ambition, it seems, is to make the most over-the-top, nostalgic, sugary treats imaginable.[25] It's all the best aspects of a kids' birthday party but for adults. Every visit is an experience. The service is informal, warm, and lovely. I adore it, and, to top it off, my sister gets her hospitality fix working there from time to time. So, I often pop in with my kids when we want to meet up and spoil ourselves.

The problem is that I tend to moderate my sugar intake. So, I usually get myself a perfect cup of coffee and enjoy indulging my grown-up kids, while I gaze longingly and admiringly at the sweet creations behind the counter from afar. One day, I said to my sister, 'You know what the owner should do? They should make a sugar-free option. It's a growing trend; there are loads of great products now...'

What an idiot.

This is a small, purpose-led café whose whole identity – its soul – revolves around indulgence. That's the whole point. This business knows exactly who it's for, and what it's here to do: spoil people. That's the mission. And it already serves me; it already gives me joy. I don't need it to do anything more. It's there for a particular moment in my life, not every day. That's the beauty of it. The truth is, I'm not their ideal customer. My adult children and the rest of their brilliantly defined tribe are. They don't need to further cater to me. If they did, all they would achieve is dilution. The experience would lose the clarity and joy that make it special. It would add pressure and overwhelm for the owner.

Before moving on to anything else, you need to know what you want and need from your business and why you're doing this. Without that clarity, the temptation to compromise will creep in, and you won't have a strong enough reason to say no. Take your time with figuring this out. Step back and use whatever format works for you, because this part is worth getting right.

## When business partnerships drift

As we discussed earlier, this work becomes even more important when multiple people are running the business. It's easy to assume that you already understand what your business partner needs and wants because you're similar, know each other well, co-wrote the business plan, or even operate different parts of the business. You might assume that both of your needs will naturally be met without doing this work. That's rarely the case.

In my first business, there were three of us, friends from university. I had known one since school. We'd grown up together, shared ideas and ambitions, and it felt natural to do it together. We did what we were supposed to do: planned for the worst, signed partnership agreements, and respected each other's strengths. We thought we had covered everything, but in all the excitement, we never stopped to uncover where we didn't align.

After spending years getting the business off the ground, within six months of opening, we realised we were pulling in different directions. It wasn't dramatic; we were simply incompatible. In a small business, our differences became impossible to ignore. We closed the partnership quickly, and we didn't speak again for ten years.

We've since made peace and, between us, we've opened ten more venues, but I've often wondered what we might have built together if we'd done the real work upfront. If we'd articulated our values, been honest about what we needed, and taken time to check that our hopes and definitions of success matched. The truth is, we had the talent and the vision, but we weren't aligned enough.

Every business starts from this point – the seed of purpose – with concentric circles forming around you. The business, the team, your customers and suppliers, your brand and your reputation – they are all built on that initial point. Being an entrepreneur is hard work. There's a reason not everyone is cut out for it. But it offers rewards, the most important of which is creating a business that works for you. Be intentional about that. And remember: it's about you. I'm not suggesting you need to be physically at the centre of everything all the time. In fact, many of my businesses have been purposely designed not to require me to take a hands-on role.

Another of my favourite hangouts is an unassuming village café called Rustic Kitchen & Deli, which punches way above its weight.[26] It's owned by two fine-dining chefs, Tom and Lee, who were friends through work and sparked off each other. They always knew how well they worked as a team. One day, an opportunity arose for them to form a partnership and build their ideal business together.

They both have young families, and they want to be at home with them as much as possible. The whole business is shaped around the life they want and the skills they bring to the table. Each plays to his strengths, and where there are gaps, they bring others in to fill them. The menu, décor, playlist, and suppliers – everything reflects their ethos. Their personality is stamped all over the place. Even the opening times and shift patterns reflect their home lives and priorities.

They have standards and they stick to them. They don't open on Mondays, and they don't take reservations. These are non-negotiables. People tell them, time and time again, how much more money they would make if they opened that extra day. It doesn't matter to them. They have a principle. A core purpose. They're holding the line. That standard is unbroken. If they aren't tempted to break it for extra cash, imagine all the other standards they're holding firm on.

Suffice it to say, they have a huge following. There's a queue outside every day. Their social media is buzzing. Everyone wants to know what they're doing. They've had endless offers of new opportunities, but they won't compromise. They'll take the next step when it's right for them, when it fits the lives they want to build. And that might be never. They understand that if it doesn't work for them, what's the point?

They also limit their roles to the tasks only they can do. They work to their strengths. If they can pay someone else to take on a task, they do, leaving them free to focus on the parts that rely on their skills, personalities, and stories. They are brilliant at stories. So much so, they even have their own podcast, making people laugh, championing the hospitality industry, celebrating their favourite suppliers, and shining a light on those who have supported them along the way.[27] This example showcases when values shape a business from the inside out.

Once you've quietened the noise and reconnected with your personal reasons for your business, the next step is to gain clarity about who your business is really for. When you know who you're for, you also know who you're not for. That kind of clarity isn't just empowering; it's foundational. The moment you define who you serve, everything else starts to make sense. That's exactly where we're going next.

## Summary

Every great hospitality business begins with a spark – a sense of purpose, a desire to do things differently, a belief in something better. Along the way, noise starts to creep in. Expectations, comparisons, and well-meaning advice can blur your original vision. This chapter helps you find your way back.

It's a reminder that your business should reflect your values, strengths, and the life you want to build. By tuning out the noise and letting go of what everyone else is doing or saying, you create the space to trust yourself. Remember what matters. Lead with clarity and reconnect with the reason you started in the first place.

You don't need to serve everyone; you need to serve the right people. When you build everything around them, you create a niche: a place where they feel they belong. You become a beacon, allowing those people to find you, not by being louder, but by being unmistakably you.

That's how you stand out. With purpose, intention, and confidence in what you've built and who it's for.

## QUESTIONS TO CONSIDER: Stand out

Turn off the noise. Become clear about what makes you different. Own your niche.

- What parts of your offer, experience, or story make you truly different from your competitors?
- In what ways are you trying to please everyone, and what is it costing you?
- Are you running your business based on your values or based on other people's expectations?
- What would it look like to embrace your niche and say no to what doesn't fit?
- How can you help your team understand and deliver on what makes you stand out?

## SEVEN
# Define Your Identity

You've accepted you're not for everyone. Now, let's figure out who you are for. This is where stand-out businesses separate themselves from others – they design from the inside out. They have a clear identity. They know who they are, what they stand for, and who they serve. That clarity always begins with you.

In this chapter, we'll define the identity of your business. We'll reconnect with your personal 'why', revisit what makes hospitality powerful, and use that foundation to build something sustainable, meaningful, and true. When everything is anchored by a purpose, and every decision flows from it, things become simpler, clearer, and more consistent. You make decisions with confidence because everything aligns.

From there, we'll explore your business vision, mission, and values. Then, we'll define your ideal customer. Finally, we'll look at how everything else – your products, team, space, voice, and systems – flows from that clarity.

## Start with purpose

You've reconnected with your personal 'why', but what about the business? What's its purpose? At the start of this book, we discussed how hospitality businesses are about more than serving food and drink. In the last chapter, we explored how independent hospitality is never aimed at everyone. It's vital to ask who you serve and why? These two questions go hand in hand. It can feel like a chicken-and-egg situation, but purpose has to come first. Everything else builds on it.

Most entrepreneurs don't take the time to really define purpose. They run on instinct and passion. While that can carry you a long way, as the business grows more complex and the decisions pile up, instinct alone starts to waver. You begin solving problems based on urgency rather than intention. You can drift, and the business can lose its centre.

When you haven't clearly articulated your purpose, things get messy. Your message starts to blur. Team culture shifts. Customers stop feeling the magic. When everything is built around a clear purpose – and every

## DEFINE YOUR IDENTITY

decision is a direct expression of that purpose – it all aligns. You feel it. They feel it. It shows.

It's easy to think you already know the answer, especially if your business is up and running. You might think your purpose is obvious, or that it doesn't need to be written down. Trust me – doing this work matters. It's the anchor you'll refer back to, the filter for every decision, and the story your customers will connect with.

So, take a pause here. Step back from the day-to-day and ask: 'Why does this business exist?' Not, 'What do we serve?' or 'How do we do it?' The real question is, 'Why does it matter?'

That question – 'Why does it matter?' – is at the heart of *The Brand Gap*, Marty Neumeier's foundational book about brand thinking, purpose, and identity.[28] Neumeier, who has advised brands like Apple, Google, and Adobe, urges every business to answer three essential questions: 'Who are you?', 'What do you do?', and 'Why does it matter?' Neumeier's answer is clear: 'A focused brand ... knows exactly what it is, why it's different, and why people want it.'

Why do you matter to them? Because when someone walks through your door, they're not merely looking for a latte, burger, or glass of wine. They're looking for something more. Something emotional. A sense of belonging. A break. A lift. A memory. A connection.

Maybe your pub is the only place where a widower speaks to anyone all week. Maybe your café is where a local mum finally gets ten minutes to herself. Maybe your bar is where people come alive on a Friday after work, reconnecting after a week of disconnection. Maybe your B&B gives couples the space to feel like themselves again. Maybe your food truck is where friends make new traditions. Those moments – they're your purpose.

You might think you're offering lunch, but to someone else, you're offering comfort, care, celebration, safety, freedom, or joy. The food and drink are the medium; the meaning is something else entirely.

One of the most powerful purpose statements I've heard came from The Secret Pub Company, a multi-award-winning group of pubs in Nottinghamshire whose accolades include the Licensee of the Year Award and the National Pub & Bar Award.[29] I worked with them during a Kith & Kin workshop. When they got to the core of their business, they landed on: 'Places where people feel loved.'

That's it. That's the heart of everything. Not a business plan or a list of services. A feeling. A truth. A reason to exist. Imagine the kinds of decisions you would make if that purpose statement was your North Star. Imagine the culture you would build, the details you would notice, and the care you would take. That's the power of a clearly felt purpose.

Your purpose isn't about a transaction. It's about influencing how someone feels. That's the real reason people come back. That's what builds loyalty. Not 'great customer service' or 'fresh ingredients', but the feeling people get when they walk through your door, and the story they tell about why it matters.

That story starts with you.

## Clarify your vision

Your vision is the world you're working towards – the future you want to create through your business. It should feel bold, emotional, expansive. It might never be fully attained, but it gives everything direction. It's what keeps you focused when things get noisy. It's what you're building towards, even if the path changes.

For example, my vision for Kith & Kin is:

> 'A thriving, values-led independent hospitality sector where no one feels alone, and everyone can find where they belong.'

That's the world I'm working towards. Every programme, event, conversation, and piece of content is a step in that direction.

Your vision should feel meaningful to you, but it should also be significant enough to inspire others. Everything you do should be in service of it.

## Define your mission

Your mission is the practical expression of your purpose; it's the work you do every day to bring your vision to life. If your vision is the destination, your mission is the journey – it's the daily commitment, the 'how'.

Our mission at Kith & Kin is:

> 'To show independent hospitality leaders that their greatest competitive advantage is creating a sense of belonging by building businesses that people need and never want to leave.'

It's practical. It's active. It's rooted in how we work and who we're for.

Whereas your vision stays steady, your mission may evolve as your business grows and changes. Your vision remains the constant thread, the deeper why. Your mission helps you focus, guides your decisions, and enables your team and customers to understand not only what you do, but also how you do it.

For example, as we saw with The Secret Pub Company, if your purpose is something like:

> 'A place where people feel loved.'

Then, your mission might be:

'We create spaces where everyone feels seen, welcomed, and cared for, by providing genuine hospitality, great food and drink, and small acts of everyday kindness.'

Alternatively, it might be:

'We host with heart, creating the kind of pub where laughs are loud, hugs are real, and every visit feels like catching up with old friends.'

Now imagine how that mission would affect the way you hire, the kind of training you offer, the menu you write, the music you play, and the language you use on social media. That's the power of mission. It brings your purpose to life every single day.

Here's a quick reminder of what each concept means:

- Your *purpose* is why your business exists – the emotive reason it matters.
- Your *vision* is the future you're working towards – the bigger world you want to help create.
- Your *mission* is how you're going to do it – the work you commit to doing every day to bring your vision to life.

Think of it like this: purpose is the heart, vision is the horizon, and mission is the path.

Here are four examples that showcase how these three elements – purpose, vision, and mission – can work together in real, human, and emotionally resonant ways.

### Example one: Coffee shop

- **Purpose:** A place where busy people can slow down and feel held.
- **Vision:** A city where people don't rush through their day and, instead, take the time to pause, connect, and feel human again.
- **Mission:** To serve exceptional, ethically sourced coffee with heartfelt service in spaces designed to help people pause, breathe, and feel present.

### Example two: Boutique B&B

- **Purpose:** A space that helps couples reconnect with each other and themselves.
- **Vision:** A world where rest is honoured, not earned.
- **Mission:** To offer beautiful, thoughtful stays in peaceful settings, with everything guests need to

breathe deeply, slow down, and feel at home with themselves and each other.

## Example three: Street food brand

- **Purpose:** Joy, flavour, and a bit of mischief in every bite.
- **Vision:** A UK-wide street food scene full of personality, creativity, and independent flavour.
- **Mission:** To serve bold, handmade food with humour and hustle, not taking itself too seriously and popping up wherever the fun is.

## Example four: Wine bar

- **Purpose:** To make good wine feel less intimidating and more joyful.
- **Vision:** A culture where wine is savoured, shared, and stripped of snobbery.
- **Mission:** To champion small producers and serve approachable, exciting wines with warmth, curiosity, and no pretence.

Each of the above examples is simple, specific, and true to the people behind it. They don't try to sound clever; they try to sound clear. That's what makes them powerful.

## Clarify your values

If your purpose is why you exist, and your mission is how you deliver on that purpose, then your values shape how it feels. Values are the emotional thread that runs through your business. They show up in the way you greet customers, the choices you make under pressure, the things you protect, and the way your team behaves when you're not in the room.

They are your boundaries. Your beliefs in action. The invisible thread that ties your business together. They're also deeply personal, especially in independent hospitality, where who you are is often inseparable from what you've built. That's not a flaw; it's a strength.

Ask yourself:

- What do I care about most?
- What will I never compromise on?
- What should people feel when they experience our work?

Those are your values. Write them down. Share them. Build from there.

## Design your customers

Once your purpose, vision, and mission are clear and you know what you value, you can move on to the next step: defining your customers. I don't mean gaining a general sense; I mean really knowing them. Understanding who you're for, what they care about, and how they experience your business. This is one of the most powerful things you can do, not only for your marketing but for every decision you make.

If you're already operating, you've probably developed a sense of who your best customers are. The ones who spend well, visit often, cause the least hassle, and bring their friends. The ones who get you. The ones you love seeing walk through the door. They are your tribe. They're already emotionally invested. They don't merely like what you do; they feel like they belong there.

If you're a new business, you have the opportunity to design who those people are. You can choose the kinds of customers you want to attract and build for them from the start.

Either way, this is the moment to get specific. Once you understand exactly who you're for, everything else becomes easier. It will shape your menu, tone, pricing, design, opening hours, playlists, team culture... everything. Equally importantly, it helps you say no. No to the wrong people, the wrong feedback, and the wrong opportunities.

This is where customer avatars are useful. Don't just picture a blurry demographic; make them real. Give them names. Know where they live, their jobs, and how they spend their weekends. Know their age, values, priorities, daily frustrations, and secret indulgences. Know which brands they love, what podcasts they listen to, and what makes them feel seen. The better you know them, the better you can serve them, and the more naturally they'll fall in love with what you do. It stops being about selling and starts being about belonging.

Let's say you run a rural pub and your ideal customer is a family with young kids. They love relaxed Sundays, generous roasts, and friendly service. They want to feel welcome to bring their children, no matter how noisy or messy it gets. You know they're juggling work, childcare, and the mental load, and they're looking for a break. So, you design for that. Spacious tables. Highchairs. Easy online booking. Warm, approachable staff. A safe corner for kids to play. Suddenly, it's not just about lunch; it's about relief, comfort, and care.

Perhaps your ideal guest is a creative thirty-something woman in a city who wants to feel inspired, connected, and proud of where she spends her money. She loves sustainability, beautiful spaces, thoughtful menus, and great storytelling. You speak her language. You create a venue that's full of texture and soul. Your brand reflects her values, and your social media gives her something to share with others. You're not just another place to eat; you're part of her identity.

Here's a powerful side note: this exercise also works for recruitment. In the same way as you define your ideal customer, you can define your ideal team. What kind of people thrive in your business? What do they care about? What values do they live by? What do they need from you as a leader, and what do you need from them? When you are clear about these, recruitment becomes less about CVs and more about fit. You attract people who align with your culture, energy, and purpose, and who are more likely to stay, contribute, and grow.

## Let your values lead

Ultimately, this is about values. Your customer avatar shouldn't merely match what you sell; it should align with what you believe. Your values are the foundation of who you attract, how you serve them, how you speak to them, and what you offer. Even more importantly, your values help you decide what you don't offer. What you don't compromise on. What you say no to.

That's the magic of alignment. The moment your values align with theirs, you stop being one of many options, and you become the obvious choice. Your business becomes more than just a venue; it becomes a home. People don't just visit homes once; they return repeatedly, tell their friends about them, and fight to protect them.

So, get personal. Get specific. Know your people. Then, build something they'll never want to leave. If you would like help with designing your customer avatar, I've included a guide in the Resources list at the end of the book with all the prompts I use with clients, from the basics like age and income to the deeper stuff like values, frustrations, and what makes them feel at home. Use it. Make them real.

## Build from alignment

You know who they are. You know why you matter to them. Now, you can design your entire business around them. Suddenly, every decision gets simpler. You're no longer guessing or reacting. You're not building for everyone; you're building for someone. Someone who matters. Someone who already loves what you do and wants more of it. Every choice becomes an opportunity to delight that person – to make them feel seen, welcomed, and at home.

You know what to put on the menu, what to stock behind the bar, and what music to play and at what volume. You know the décor, artwork, lighting, furniture, uniforms, and signage. You know the welcome, language, tone of voice, and social media captions. You know your events, loyalty strategy, booking process, feedback system, pricing, portion sizes, waste policy, and sustainability standards. You know how to recruit, whom to promote, what to say no to, and

## DEFINE YOUR IDENTITY

what to never compromise on. You know how to train your team, which behaviours to reward, and what energy to protect.

You know what to preserve and what to let go. You've built a business that stands for something, and that's what makes it strong. Ask yourself: Does it align with your purpose? Does it bring you closer to your vision? If the answer's yes, do more of it. If it doesn't, let it go.

That noise we spoke about earlier? It's quieter now because you're no longer reacting to trends or chasing competitors. You're building from the inside out, grounded in clarity, guided by purpose, and shaped by who you truly want to serve. And the best part? You're not just running a business any more; you're creating belonging. You've got a mission you care about. A message that resonates. A beacon that calls your people home. That kind of clarity doesn't just help you stand out; it helps people find their way in. The moment someone walks through your door and thinks, 'This is for me' – that's when belonging begins. In independent hospitality, belonging isn't just a feeling; it's your biggest competitive advantage.

Before you move on, capture this clarity. Write it down, not only for yourself, but also so that others can build upon it too. If it's going to shape your training, decisions, and culture, it needs to be clear. No grey areas. No guesswork. Keep it relevant, real, and ready to use, whether you're welcoming a new team member, briefing a supplier, or sharing your story with someone who might help you grow. What you've uncovered here is gold. Protect it. Systemise it. Let it lead.

## Summary

This chapter reminded you that stand-out businesses are built from the inside out. They know who they are, what they stand for, and who they serve. They're not shaped by trends or other people's opinions, but rather by purpose, values, and truth.

You reconnected with your personal why, clarified the purpose of your business, and started seeing every decision through that lens. Once you're grounded in purpose, everything gets simpler. You're no longer chasing what others are doing; you're building something that's truly yours.

You defined your vision: the world you want to help create. You outlined your mission: the work you do every day to get there. You clarified your values: the beliefs that guide how your business feels, acts, and leads. From there, you dug deep to define the people you're here for. You moved beyond assumptions towards truly understanding them – their lives, values, and desires. When you build for them, you stop trying to please everyone, and you become a beacon guiding the right customers to you.

That's what alignment looks like. Your products, team, tone, and systems, can all be shaped by purpose and designed for the people who matter most. That's how you stop the noise. That's how you grow with clarity. That's how you build a business that not only stands out but stands for something.

Now, every decision is simple. Does it move you closer to your vision? Does it align with your purpose? If yes, do more of it. If not, let it go. You're not just running a business; you're creating a place where people want to belong.

---

**QUESTIONS TO CONSIDER: Define your identity**

Know who you are. Build a business rooted in purpose, clarity, and emotional alignment.

- Why did you start this business, and why does it still matter to you today?
- Who is your ideal customer, and how clearly have you designed your business for them?
- What emotional need are you meeting for your team and customers?
- Does your current offer, experience, and brand identity reflect your values and vision?
- What's your mission, and how often do you share it with your team?

---

## EIGHT
# Build Belonging

We've spent time defining your identity. We've done the internal work of clarifying who you are, what you stand for, and who you're here to serve. Next, we step into the emotional space that brings it all to life: belonging. This chapter explores how to build a sense of belonging for your customers, your team, and yourself.

Every friendship group is a community. Every family is part of one. There are workplace communities, online communities, and creative communities. Every hospitality business – whether it's a café, restaurant, B&B, or cocktail bar – is serving a community. A tribe. This is what you are building. When we talk about community, we're talking about connection. A group of people connected by something deeper than food or drink. A group that shares something: their values, beliefs, and how they see the world. A place where people feel seen, understood, and welcome.

Let's remind ourselves how we got here. So far, we've discussed the challenges facing the hospitality industry today. There's the sense of overwhelm due to the complexity of the industry, pressure from customers who seem less engaged, and teams that feel more demanding. Both customers and teams can feel more transactional than they used to, and they expect more from every interaction.

Through these conversations, we've uncovered something deeper. Despite the demands, customers and teams still crave a sense of belonging. They're more switched on than ever. They recognise their worth, and they know yours too. They'll tell you how they feel, either explicitly or by walking out. It's possible to create surface-level engagement, such as five-star reviews, a happy team, and curated experiences, but real commitment often feels elusive. The very people your business is built for seem less loyal than they once were, and you're right to notice that.

Yet, people are still searching for something meaningful. Our teams may appear transactional, but many are looking for work that matters. It's no longer enough to pay well or offer a few perks. They want to be part of something they believe in. They want to feel proud of where they work. They want their energy to count for something.

This is why we're seeing more polarised views, cause-driven behaviour, and values-led decision-making. It's also why younger generations, especially Gen Z, are increasingly prioritising environmental and ethical values, choosing brands that align with their beliefs, expecting authenticity and transparency from leadership, demanding flexible and mentally supportive workplaces, and actively engaging in social change and activism.

## When everything clicks

Our customers are not merely coming out to eat or drink. They're looking for something more profound. As Maslow's hierarchy of needs explains, food and water meet our most basic requirements, but hospitality reaches far beyond survival. At its best, it fulfils higher needs like belonging (feeling connected and part of something), esteem (being recognised, respected, and valued), and self-actualisation (being inspired, growing, and experiencing life in full colour).

Tony Robbins' model of the six human needs echoes this. They are six needs that hospitality is uniquely placed to meet: certainty (comfort, routine, safety), variety (novelty, adventure, surprise), significance (feeling important, unique, valued), connection and love (human bonds, shared experience), growth (learning, developing, becoming more), and contribution (giving back, making a difference). Every hospitality experience has the potential to meet each of those needs. When you meet them – deeply, meaningfully – for your team and your customers, something shifts. You stop selling products and start building belief, loyalty, and a sense of belonging. The kind that lasts.

We've also talked about leadership. Setting high standards for yourself and your business is like dropping a pebble in a pond, with concentric circles rippling outwards. We explored why starting with you – understanding your needs, ambitions, and emotional drivers – has a direct impact on how your business is structured. We looked at how designing your target customer base to fit your business involves first understanding the purpose of your business, emotionally engaging with that purpose, and building around it.

You have a purpose, and it's not about sticking a piece of A4 paper on the wall that says, 'We are here to serve our customers great food and drink with a smile.' Sure, that's the transaction, but where's the emotion? Where's the fire in the belly? The bit that motivates people to go above and beyond, not because they have to, but because it means something. Because it's worth it.

A mission should inspire you to make a sacrifice for it, not because you're a martyr, but because you care. It's how you're going to change the world. Not in a grand, sweeping way, but one person, one interaction at a time. A smile and eye contact can be written into your training manuals, but what then? When McDonald's brought 'Have a nice day' to the UK, we rolled our eyes. Not because we didn't like the sentiment, but because it felt forced. We knew, instinctively, that it wasn't genuine. It became a joke. A line in a script.

Your customers are clever. They know the difference between a real smile and a trained one. Humans are brilliant at spotting genuineness. You can't fake kindness. That's why, when I work with operators to rediscover their purpose and translate it into something they can live by, it's powerful. There's a moment when it clicks – when they find the words they truly believe in. The words they can take back to their teams. That clarity shifts everything.

You saw examples in the last chapter of real purpose statements and meaningful missions from operators who know who they are and who they serve. They might sound simple, but when they're true, they change everything. A good mission doesn't have to be poetic; it has to be real. I'm telling you, this is the true magic. This is the biggest shift you'll see. It's the culmination of all your hard work. When you have a mission you're emotionally engaged with – one that makes sense, brings everything together, and you can communicate through every micro-interaction – you become a leader on a mission.

A leader on a mission inspires a team, and a team – a tribe – on a mission is intoxicating. Everyone wants to join in. You see it in every walk of life. Every movement, every march. People rally behind a cause, a shared belief. Think about: climate activists cleaning beaches; football fans chanting from the stands; nurses striking not only for better pay but for dignity; queues outside venues that stand for something; and school kids walking out for climate justice. Humans are wired to move in sync with others who care about the same things.

This is that moment in your business. The moment it all clicks. When the noise quiets. When people stop clocking in and start showing up. We spoke earlier about how challenging it has become to engage teams in a meaningful way; well, this is it. This is what they've been waiting for. This is what they want to belong to. They're part of the ripple.

If you can inspire them with your mission, everything becomes simpler. Training lands faster. They need less input from you. They start making it work on their own. They share knowledge. They go above and beyond. They support each other. They lift each other up. They free up your time. Standards rise naturally. Suddenly, you're not pushing people uphill; you have a team that is moving in the same direction for the same reason. They become committed, loyal, and energised.

This is what they've always needed from you – clarity, purpose, and belief (not perfection or constant instruction). Once you give them what they need, everything changes. When your team is lit up – aligned, energised, emotionally invested – something even bigger happens. That energy doesn't stop with them; it reaches your customers, too. It ripples into the welcome, the atmosphere, and the way people feel when they walk through your doors. This builds belonging.

To build a thriving hospitality business, you need customers who discover you, love you, and come back again and again. They don't fixate on the price because you're meeting so many of their other needs, making the cost worthwhile. They feel seen and cared for. Everyone else in the room feels like their type of people, too. They feel like they could order anything off the menu and want to come back for the rest. The playlist feels like it was made for them. The décor matches their dream home. The lighting is perfect. The chairs are comfortable. The temperature's spot on. It's like Goldilocks found Baby Bear's bed. They could stay all day.

You know what people are always saying? How hard it is to find the right place. Everyone's looking for it. A place where they feel at home. Somewhere that gets them. Places like that are rare, but when you build around purpose, values, and belonging, that's exactly what you become. When they find their place, they don't keep it to themselves. They tell everyone. They talk to their friends, colleagues, and family. They want to bring them along because they know they'll love it too. They want to share the place that makes them feel seen.

Even so, not everyone will get it. When someone doesn't feel the mission or actively resists it, that misalignment quickly becomes clear.

## When the team doesn't belong

You recruit someone who seems perfect on paper: they say all the right things and perform brilliantly during a trial shift. You're hopeful, maybe even relieved. But as time goes on, something isn't sitting right.

You start communicating the mission more clearly. The rest of the team responds – engaged, excited, connecting the dots. They see that service isn't just about a smile or a script; it's about recognising people, creating moments, and being kind. But this one team member? They roll their eyes. They show up late. They undermine. They dismiss your standards.

They whisper about others and work to a different agenda.

As a good leader, you do the work. You take responsibility. You coach. You communicate clearly. You give them chances. You hope, but nothing changes. Eventually, you realise that they're not merely disengaged, they're actively undermining what you're trying to build. It's one of the hardest moments in leadership – when you have to remove someone you like and once trusted for the sake of your team.

I've lived this myself. One of the hardest decisions I ever made was letting go of a manager who had helped me build something special. We'd worked together for years. I supported him through a personal hardship, and when things settled, something had shifted. He no longer aligned with the business or with me. He wanted control. He resisted direction. Gradually, his influence became toxic. I felt it. The team felt it.

Letting him go was heartbreaking. I lost a colleague, confidante, and friend. He walked away filled with resentment. Now, he runs an international events company. He was ready for something bigger. Even though it hurt, the end of that chapter made space for us both to do more.

Set your standards high and stick to them. If it isn't working, let it go.

## Let go to make space

Don't cling on to every customer either. There are millions of people in the world, and realistically, not everyone is your audience. You don't need to be liked by all. Within your local reach, how many people are there, and how many do you actually need to make your business thrive?

There are plenty of fish in the sea. If it's not a good match, let it go. When you stop chasing the wrong fit, you create space for the right ones – the people who do belong and will build something meaningful with you.

I was about to tell you about my favourite business, but as I started writing, I realised they're all my favourites for different reasons. Each had different strengths. However, one particular city centre bar was especially meaningful. It wasn't my first business, so I had experience and, this time, I built with intention. The area had just been rebranded the 'cultural quarter', with investment going into a theatre and an arts centre.

Despite the regeneration, it still lacked heart. That's what I set out to build. My mission was simple: to become the heart of the cultural quarter. That wasn't merely a tagline. It became the lens through which we made every decision. The décor was homemade and cosy, with second-hand furniture, set in a quirky, triangular building that had once stood empty. Picture something like the New York Flatiron Building, filled with vintage sofas, candlelight, and jam jar cocktails. It felt warm, relaxed, and real.

If we were going to be the heart of the quarter, we had to be more than a bar. We opened up side rooms and the cellar for anyone to use, completely free. We wanted to be a canvas for people's lives. Over time, that's exactly what we became. Knitting clubs, record clubs, book launches, birthdays, weddings, and wakes. We were the green room for the theatre and the after-party for sold-out shows. A home for local creatives, musicians, and actors. People didn't just come for a drink; they came to belong.

They tested ideas at our tables. They wrote business plans, launched startups, and held their first meetings, often with nothing more than a coffee and a notepad. Before co-working became a trend, we were the office away from the office. A place for the conversations that didn't fit anywhere else. Somewhere that felt safe, human, and real.

We hosted philosophy meet-ups, informal lectures, and choir rehearsals. Festival lineups were dreamed up there and debated well into the night. We played host to political groups, fringe casts, first-time founders, and zine-makers. Movements were born. Culture unfolded. Ideas took flight.

I realised we weren't just serving drinks; we were hosting new beginnings. A backdrop for boldness.

A place where stories started, sparks caught, and the next chapter of people's lives quietly began. Every emotion and kind of human moment lived within those walls.

All I did was set out with a mission that others believed in and ran with. Great things become even greater than the sum of their parts. We created the space, served with generosity and kindness, and we built a tribe. We became a beacon, and that beacon drew others in.

## Not all customers are equal: Understanding loyalty

When I used to train my teams, I needed a tool to emphasise an important point that is often missed: not all customers are equal. Customers behave and feel differently. If we want to have an impact, we need to recognise who they are and our individual objectives for each one.

So, I created the Kith & Kin Customer Loyalty Map inspired by classic customer loyalty models but reimagined through the lens of independent hospitality. I've used it to train every team I've worked with. It has stuck because it helps explain, in simple terms, how customers behave, and how we often end up focusing on the wrong ones.

BUILD BELONGING

The model maps customers based on two factors: their level of satisfaction and their loyalty. The results aren't always what you would expect.

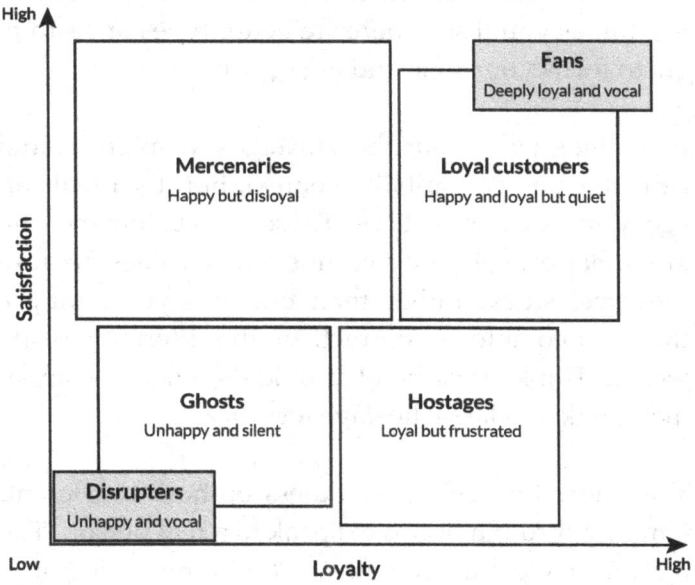

*The Kith & Kin Customer Loyalty Map*

First, let's start with the **Mercenaries**. These customers are highly satisfied, but they have no loyalty. They shop around for deals, bring a voucher, or choose you because you were the cheapest or most convenient option that day. You might deliver an amazing experience, and they might even leave a glowing five-star review, but they won't be back.

This is exactly why discounting rarely works to attract new customers – you're not building a relationship.

137

You're attracting people who aren't loyal anywhere. They're driven by price, novelty, and convenience. Some may not feel the need to belong anywhere in particular. You might convert a few into loyal customers, but as you'll see, there are better types of customers to focus your time and energy on.

Next, let's talk about the **Hostages**. It might sound ridiculous in a hospitality context, but it's a real category in other industries. These are customers who are unhappy, yet they continue to come back because they feel stuck, rather than out of loyalty. Maybe they're tied into a contract, or the alternatives are worse. Think broadband providers, energy companies, banks... classic hostage territory.

You know the feeling – endless on-hold music and jumping through hoops to speak to a real person. The reason they get away with it? You're not going anywhere. You're a hostage. They can afford to care less, because leaving is hard. In independent hospitality, that doesn't exist. Our customers can walk out and never return – and they often do. So, while this concept is useful to understand, it's not one we can rely on. We can't trap customers. We have to attract them and keep them.

Then, we have the **Ghosts**. These are the customers who quietly drift away. Something doesn't land or feels off, but they don't complain; they just don't come back. Maybe they smiled as they left. Maybe they assured you everything was fine when you checked in with them. But the truth is, they weren't happy. They didn't feel seen. They didn't feel it mattered.

That's why your team needs to be brave. They need to be trained to spot discomfort and take action. When they do – when they catch it in the moment – those almost-lost customers can become some of your most loyal. It's not about perfection; it's about care.

Then, there are the **Disrupters**. You've met them. They are the customers who want you to know they're not happy. They call for a manager. They complain loudly. They blast you in a review. They might even take to social media. Their goal? To make noise. To be right. Sometimes, to do damage.

Occasionally, their complaint is justified. Mistakes happen. When they do, it's our job to take responsibility, listen with care, and put things right. That can be powerful. If handled well, a Disrupter can be transformed into one of your most loyal customers. They want to feel seen, heard, and important. Sometimes they need their ego massaged and their frustration acknowledged. Fair enough, give it a go.

At other times, they're just mean. They're not looking for resolution; they're looking for control. In those cases, you have permission to let them go. Don't lose sleep over it. Don't waste hours crafting the perfect reply. If they're not part of your tribe, that's OK.

Remember: if they treat you and your team that way, they probably treat others the same. Most of your other customers will recognise this too. People can spot bad behaviour for what it is. What matters is recognising the difference and responding with the clarity and confidence that come from knowing who you are and who you're here for.

Now, let's talk about your happy customers – your **Loyal Customers**. They are the people who really like you. They're satisfied, they keep coming back, and they bring a lovely sense of ease. They know you, and you probably know them. They're reliable, low-drama, and steady. Every hospitality business has them, and they're a joy to serve.

But here's the risk: if you're stuck in a transactional mindset, these customers can be overlooked. They're not demanding or shouting. They're showing up, and they're the foundation of your business. Don't take them for granted.

Finally, there are the **Fans**. These are the customers who love you. They don't just enjoy your business, they believe in it. They feel emotionally connected. They align with your values, even if you've never spelled them out. They forgive the odd mistake. They give generous, thoughtful feedback. They spend well. They bring their friends. They advocate for you without needing to be asked. They're part of your tribe, and they help spread the word.

## BUILD BELONGING

If you're building a business rooted in purpose, connection, and belonging, these are your people. They're the dream. When you have Fans, everything is easier. They become part of your story. They do your marketing for you. Even better, they attract more people like them.

That's the difference between a customer and a fan. Customers think with their heads; fans feel with their hearts. Customers compare, weigh up the options, and look for value. Fans don't; they already know they belong.

That's why some brands feel like movements. It's why people queue overnight for a new iPhone. It's why they get tattoos of logos on their bodies. It's why, when something truly resonates, price becomes almost irrelevant. Fans don't care about the cost. Consider the chaos when Oasis announced their reunion tour. Tickets sold out within minutes. There wasn't outrage about the price, but rather that people couldn't get a ticket. Fans don't care about the cost. They just want to be there. That's the power of emotional connection. Other customers will leave when a better offer comes along, but a fan? A fan is with you. They'll follow you anywhere.

Let the Mercenaries go. They were never going to stay. They came for a deal, a moment, a mood, and that's OK. You don't need them to grow something meaningful. Don't let the Disrupters get you down. Some can be turned around, and with care, confidence, and grace, they might just become your loudest advocates. The others? They're there to stir the pot, and that says more about them than it does about you. Focus instead on the customers who recognise what you're building.

If you really want to have fun – and only because it is fun, not because it's another task – then play at transforming Disrupters, Ghosts, and Loyal Customers into Fans. Know your ideal customer, recognise them when they come in, and understand what they need from you. Then watch that group of Fans grow steadily, right alongside your business. When that happens, it's something else entirely. The truth is, Fans are the most valuable people in your business; they're proof that you've built something meaningful and real. Something that truly matters. Those Fans aren't just your ideal customers. Each is a version of your avatar. They make your business simple.

They're called Fans because they love you, and they can't help but spread the word. They do it through emotional engagement by telling stories. Storytelling is something humans love above anything else. When people tell stories about you – real stories, rooted in feeling and meaning – then what you've built becomes part of their lives. Not just a place they visited, but a place they carry with them.

## Summary

You did the work to define who you are. This chapter shows you how to bring that to life by creating belonging. Belonging is strategic. It's the reason your customers return, your team stays, and your culture grows stronger with every interaction.

In this chapter, you saw that people don't merely crave good service; they seek connection. Customers come back because they feel seen, understood, and valued. Teams give more when they feel part of something they believe in. You lead better when you're clear about what you stand for and who you're building it for.

You were reminded that not everyone will belong. That's not a failure; that's the work. Protecting your mission, standards, and culture will help you grow something that lasts. That means holding firm, letting go when it's time, and trusting that the right people – your people – will find you. Because when people belong, they stay. They share. They advocate. They bring others with them. They don't just become customers; they become part of your story. In a world overwhelmed with choice and noise, this kind of emotional connection is the edge.

You explored the emotional power of loyalty and the customer loyalty map that helps you stop chasing the wrong people. You learned that not all customers are equal: Mercenaries, Disrupters, and Ghosts will come and go, but Fans will fuel your future. They're your tribe and, when you build a business around them, everything gets simpler.

You've built your foundation. Now you're building your tribe. Let that be your ripple. That is your advantage.

---

**QUESTIONS TO CONSIDER: Build belonging**

Create an emotional connection and foster loyalty by building a culture and customer experience that makes people feel valued.

- Who in your business (team or customer) already feels like they belong? How do you know?
- What emotions do you want people to feel consistently when they interact with your business?
- Are your standards and values visible in the small details of the customer and team experience?
- What behaviours are you currently tolerating that undermine your culture of belonging?
- What could you do this week to deepen the connection with your team or your customers?

---

## NINE
# Tell A Great Story

Humans don't remember facts. We remember the stories we tell about those facts. Every moment of our lives is shaped by a narrative – what we believe about the world, what we say about ourselves, and what we share with others. It's how we connect, build trust, and make sense of everything. We are wired for stories.

On the Kith & Kin podcast, I have the joy of listening to and sharing the stories of hospitality professionals from across the industry. When I set out, I planned each episode to be twenty minutes of sharing a journey and telling of how we fall in love with the industry. Once we start talking about our lives – our stories, the choices we've made, what we've learned about ourselves and others, and how we see and move through the world – conversations naturally run to around forty-five minutes. Even then, I'm often nudging things along or editing for time.

The truth is, we make sense of our lives through the stories we tell – narratives that weave our experiences into something meaningful. We connect with others by listening to and telling those tales. It's how we find understanding, and it's how we find meaning. Humans are driven to tell stories.

Whenever I tell the story of how I met my husband, I always remember the three hospitality venues that served as the backdrop. The image in my mind when I think of my friend's dad's wake – a huge affair attended by half the town – is of a familiar venue. When I visited my close friend after her divorce, I remember us sitting opposite each other in a particular café. I know exactly where it was, and I could probably tell you what we had. That keynote speech I gave – I remember the venue clearly, including the uniforms of the well-presented staff. Like everyone else, such moments chart my life, and each has a home in a hospitality venue.

We have patterns of communicating with ourselves and each other that take us on a journey – the highs, the lows, and the resolution. There's usually a relatable character (often ourselves), a setting (like our first pub job, or the kitchen that shaped us), a challenge or conflict (something we didn't expect or tested us), a turning point (a lesson learnt, a bold decision made), and some resolution or insight (who we became because of it, and why we stayed in this brilliant, bonkers industry). Think about it.

## Hospitality is a story bank

A hospitality business is a story bank. It's where your customers come to tell, hear, and create a story. We are the blank canvas on which lives are painted. But we are not neutral bystanders – we are the scenery, the backdrop, the setting. We are the side character, the backstory, the lighting, the mood, the moment of conflict or calm. We are the small but significant detail that gives the main plot its meaning. We give those stories richness, depth, and texture. We make them more memorable and meaningful.

The customers who truly fell in love with my venues – and felt part of our tribe – didn't have just one memory. We were home to the memories of a whole period in their lives. My first venue was where twenty-somethings starting out in their first jobs and homes met their lifelong friendship groups. It was where they met their life partners and celebrated milestone birthdays, engagements, and weddings. They came for legendary nights out, and returned for weekend brunches to reminisce and soak it all in. They brought their newborns for a first experience of the real world. They shared joy and heartbreak.

And they loved my venue – perhaps even more than I did.

Storytelling is how we emotionally engage with each other because, at its core, it's about understanding. When you tell the story of your business – why you do what you do, the values that guide you, the moments that shaped you – you invite your customer to understand you.

But storytelling isn't just about being seen. It's about seeing them, too. When you know your customer deeply – when you've done the work to understand who they are, what they care about, how they feel, and what they need – you're telling a story that shows them they belong. That's why you define your customer avatar. Not to create a marketing persona, but to make sure your story is one they'll recognise as their own. That's what they're really asking when they scroll through your feed or walk through your door: 'Do you understand me, and will I understand you?' Forget another photo of your latest burger special. They already know you sell food and drink. What they want is connection. That's what your story delivers; that's marketing.

Stories are how humans connect. They're how we share understanding. And when we feel seen and heard, or misunderstood, we respond emotionally. I can tell you, without hesitation, about a time I cried, raged, or laughed so hard I couldn't breathe. I share these moments to connect – to show empathy, express shared experience, make people smile, teach, belong, and lead. To show my understanding of what it means to be human.

Because we're all telling stories, even when we're not speaking.

## Marketing that misses the point

The big question is: why do we overlook storytelling when building our businesses and marketing? After all, marketing, though done for a particular purpose, is just another form of storytelling. It's a way of broadcasting that we're here; this is what we do. So often it misses the part that makes the biggest difference – the emotional connection with the audience.

Too often, a marketing strategy is confused with advertising and promotion. Advertising is shouting into the void – telling everyone, 'I'm here, come and see!' – on the assumption that the reason people haven't come before, or haven't been back, is simply because they didn't know about you. Just get in front of them and shout! (Apologies to all the marketers out there, I know I'm simplifying.)

The reality is that, too often, after a wonderful business has been built with heart, this approach falls flat. While it may be effective at telling people the business exists, which might work temporarily as people try something new, it doesn't stick. It has no meaning. People need more. They're looking for belonging. They're looking for that place that gets them, that knows what they need better than they do, and that cares about them and where they want to invest. That's an emotional connection. And it needs a story.

As I've built the Kith & Kin community, I've interacted with thousands of hospitality businesses on social media. My purpose is to connect with and support them, even if it's just a quick comment on a post. Often, the posts they're putting out are beautiful pictures of their venues, food, drinks, or rooms – stunning spaces and dishes, carefully posed and crafted – but I struggle to comment on them meaningfully. There are only so many ways I can say, 'Wow, that looks delicious,' 'What a gorgeous setup,' or 'That's a nice-looking room,' before I feel I lose integrity. Lovely though they may be, they all begin to blur into one. Every venue starts to look similar. Every place seems to serve 'Instagrammable' food and drinks, and even I don't have very much to say about that.

What excites me is when the people, customers, and staff come through. When, between the carefully staged shots, there's a flash of real joy or connection. A moment of laughter. A spark of something unfolding. I catch a glimpse of someone I'd love to meet, or a frame that feels like the middle of a story.

## Give customers a story to tell

As part of my team training, we used to do an exercise. By all means, give it a go. We would write on a board everything the customer valued about us: our playlist, clean toilets, speciality products, friendly staff, the welcome they received at the door, the atmosphere, us remembering their drink order, the handwritten thank-you note, the comfy chairs, the smell of fresh coffee... You get it. It's what you designed back in Chapter Seven (Define Your Identity).

Then, we put each into one of three categories: product, people, or experience. These became the points of a triangle. They were the areas of the business over which we had control, and our team could see how their day-to-day interactions influenced our customers.

The question was: how does this hang together? What's the thing that really matters to customers? Where do these three areas intersect? The answer was always: memories.

We are memory makers. Our customers leave every visit with a lasting memory. That memory becomes a story. That story becomes the basis of word-of-mouth promotion. If we can give our customers stories, they will tell them on our behalf. That becomes their reason to visit again, and the reason they bring others with them.

## Stories spread by people

The great thing about word-of-mouth promotion is that customers want to do it. Many businesses try to financially incentivise it, but that just cheapens it. Being paid for a referral misses the point. The customers who love you – the Fans – want to share about your business. The psychology behind that is far more interesting than any financial incentive. Over the years, I've noticed a clear pattern in how customers discover and adopt hospitality businesses. It always starts with a few bold explorers, grows through trusted recommendations, and eventually becomes the place 'everyone's talking about'. It's a rhythm most of us instinctively recognise – a momentum that builds person to person, one story at a time. I developed this concept into the Word-of-Mouth Wave.

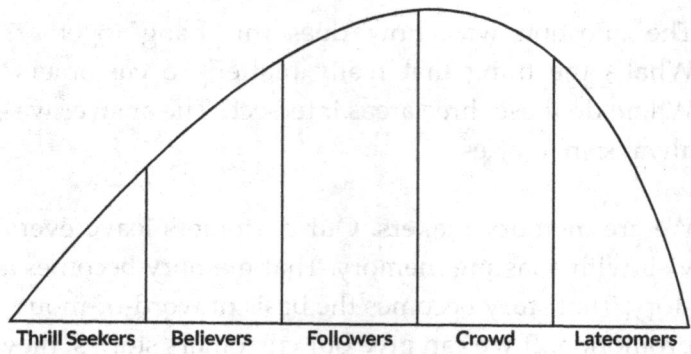

*The Word-of-Mouth Wave: How customers discover and adopt hospitality businesses*

There are five types of customers:

1. **The Thrill Seekers:** The Thrill Seekers are brave. They're the curious, up-for-anything crowd. They'll come to the opening of a crisp packet if you let them – not because they know it's good, but because they want to be first. They're drawn to newness, excitement, and the chance to say, 'I found it first.'

2. **The Believers:** The Believers are the Thrill Seekers who visit, and something clicks. They feel the vibe. They get what you're about. Once they've decided you're for them, they go and tell others. They're the early adopters of your story. The first settlers in your tribe.

3. **The Followers:** The Followers have been watching, listening, maybe even walking past. They're waiting for someone else – someone like them – to say, 'It's worth it.' When they see the Believers sharing, tagging, and raving... that's their cue. They want in. This is when you build traction.

4. **The Crowd:** Once the buzz is strong enough, and there's a sense that everyone is going, FOMO kicks in and the Crowd shows up. They might not feel deeply connected (yet), but they don't want to miss out. You've become the safe and popular choice.

5. **The Latecomers:** Cautious, sceptical, and slow to move, the Latecomers weren't easily convinced. But now they're curious. Eventually, they come – usually because someone close to them won't shut up about you. It's not the advertising that wins them over; it's the voices they repeatedly hear and trust.

The point is people adopt you and find their new 'home' through each other. Through talking. Through stories.

The Thrill Seekers might respond to advertising or buzz, but everyone else is watching and waiting. They need social proof. They need a story. Their fear runs deeper than whether it's no good. Their fear is, 'What if I go, and no one else does?' What if they get up on the dance floor, bust some serious moves, and everyone just stares?

Once someone decides you are for them, they are driven to go out and tell everyone about you. They want everyone to agree that you really are the next big thing – that their judgement and taste were right. They do this by making sure everyone else becomes your customer, too.

Financially incentivising this process only undermines it. It tells people that you're only about the financial transaction; that all they mean to you is pound signs. You make them feel like you don't really see them.

Word of mouth can be a slow and frustrating process, but it is by far the most effective, sustainable, and long-term strategy you have. The way to do it is by following the Five Pillars.

Create a sense of belonging. Build a business that targets the right customer. Design the business for them and then blow them away with your consistently high standards. Make sure they know that you get them and that they belong with you. Transition them from Loyal Customer to Fan.

Give them stories to tell. Make it easy for them to find reasons to talk about you. Give them social media content that warrants genuine comment. Let them get to know you and your team.

In hospitality, we do more than serve food and drink. We create moments. Moments that become memories, and memories that become stories. And stories – they are what people take with them when they leave.

Think about your favourite memories. They're not bullet points or photos; they're stories. The time you were made to feel special. The surprise gesture. The giggles around the table. The quiet kindness of a barista who noticed you were having a hard day and remembered your order from before. The time your kids were welcomed like VIPs. The night everything felt right. Those moments didn't happen by chance. They happened because someone cared. Someone showed up fully and gave you something real. That's the power of story. And that's the power of you.

Hospitality is a storytelling industry. When people visit your venue, they enter a stage where you are the host of the show. It's not scripted or fake. It involves real, human connection. Your job is to create a story people want to step into, live in, and carry home. Every touchpoint tells a tale, from your lighting and music to your welcome, team, tone of voice, and presence.

The flipside is that if you're not telling your story intentionally, people will create one. It just might not be the story you want them to tell.

## People buy from people

To bring together everything we've explored, I want to close by zooming in on the one thing that makes your business truly unforgettable: your personal story.

I'm a natural introvert, and I know that being front and centre is hard for some people. But it is worth considering, because you and your personal brand are a superpower. Too often, business owners hide behind their logo and business personality. I certainly did. For nearly eighteen years of running my businesses, I only ever spoke as the business and for the business. I kept myself extremely private. Over the years, I discovered that letting people get to know me made the biggest difference to my business.

## TELL A GREAT STORY

After attending a networking event full of other businesspeople, nearly everyone I spoke with booked a table or came for a drink at my venue that day. It was magic. People want to buy from people. They want to spend their money with people they know, like, and trust. While we could debate how well someone might know me from a brief meeting or from seeing my face and a short caption on a social media post, they still know more about my venue than they do about most others. And if I seem like someone they might like, then I beat the faceless corporations every time.

As an independent hospitality business, you are your biggest marketing asset. Tell your story. That's why this final part of your business model – the part that makes you unforgettable – is not just about great service or a quality product; it's about being known. Seen. Recognised. Trusted. It's about stepping into your personal brand.

People don't buy from logos. Let's be honest, no one emotionally connects with a logo. No one says, 'Oh, I love this font – they must really understand me.' We fall in love with people. We fall in love with founders who care, baristas who remember our names, teams that radiate pride and purpose, and brands that feel human. People who we feel understand us, and who we, in turn, understand.

In independent hospitality, your secret weapon is you – your face, your voice, your reason why. You are the magic ingredient that chain businesses will never be able to copy. Yet so many of us hide behind our brand. We post perfect pictures of flat whites and cocktails, but we don't show the people who made them. We write captions in the third person and use the royal 'we' instead of saying, 'Hi, this is me, and this is why this matters.' We're not trying to be influencers, but we're trying to build a connection. The moment you start to share your real story and show up with honesty and heart, everything shifts. People start to feel something, and that feeling is the beginning of loyalty.

And if you're shy? You don't need to do a dance on TikTok. You don't need to go live every day. You don't even need to post selfies if it doesn't feel right. But you do need to show up authentically. Start by sharing your story on your website – a simple paragraph about why you opened, what you care about, and who you're here to serve. A picture of you with your team. Your values, in your own words. Speak in your voice on your site, social media, everywhere. Even if it's short, let it sound like you: a person, not a brand.

You've done the work now. You know why this matters to you. Share that. Everyone has a story about why they fell in love with the industry and chose this path. Let people connect with it.

If you have team members who love the camera, use them too, but be mindful that you're giving your power away to someone who may only be part of your journey for a short time. Make sure your story remains at the heart of it all, because your story is your leadership. Your reason why is your purpose. When you lead with that, people follow.

## The ripple effect of storytelling

Remember the pebble in the pond? You are at the centre. Your story sends out the first ripple. Your team is the next. Then your customers. Then your wider community. Then, finally, the market. If your voice isn't there at the start, the ripple fades fast. When your story is clear, authentic, and connected to your purpose, those ripples travel far. They touch people you'll never meet. They create an impact long after the bill is paid. They build a business that matters.

I was recently asked to share one special hospitality moment for an article: a heartwarming story, a moment of laughter, or a random act of kindness. I said I couldn't choose just one. Not because I didn't have any, but because there were simply too many to choose from. When you're the operator, these moments become everyday; you're surrounded by them. But to the customer, they are anything but ordinary. They're rare, meaningful, and personal. They're moments they'll talk about for years. We're lucky enough to witness them on every shift. For them, it's the memory they carry home.

Still, as I sent that response about the article, a memory did gently surface – one that reminded me why I love this work. At the pub, we hosted an outdoor cinema. It was a glorious bank holiday – one of those golden afternoons that felt gentle and unhurried for the families who joined us, even though, behind the scenes, it was a huge and busy event. I paused for a moment and looked out across the garden. A group of young children sat together on picnic blankets, totally enthralled, watching Frozen on the huge outdoor screen. Beside them, in costume and completely in character, sat a real-life Elsa. It was a perfect, unscripted piece of magic. I watched a lifelong memory form right before my eyes.

In hospitality, we create the setting for memories to be made and stories to begin. Often, we don't even realise we're doing it. Storytelling isn't just a marketing tool – it's a leadership tool, a trust builder, the heartbeat of belonging.

Your story matters. And it's time to tell it. When people believe in your story, they'll share it. They'll carry it with them. They'll bring others home.

## Summary

Hospitality is where stories happen. We are the backdrop of people's lives – the setting for memories they'll talk about for years to come. This chapter explored how everything we do, from the lighting to the welcome, becomes part of someone's story. It's those stories, not our menus or interiors, that people carry home.

You've learned that storytelling isn't separate from marketing; it's what makes it meaningful. It's how we build an emotional connection and help people feel seen. It's how we move from transaction to trust.

You saw that people don't fall in love with logos; they fall in love with people – founders who care, teams who connect, and places that feel like they were made for them. When that happens, they tell others. Word of mouth isn't something you can force. It's something you earn by giving people moments worth remembering and stories worth sharing.

---

**QUESTIONS TO CONSIDER: Tell a great story**

Use your personal brand, values, and storytelling to foster emotional resonance and build a brand people believe in.

- What's the story behind your business, and are you telling it?
- Where are you hiding behind your logo instead of showing your face and voice?
- Are you sharing the stories of your team, customers, or community in a way that reflects your values?

- What memories are your customers making, and how can you give them more reasons to talk about you?
- What's one story you could tell this week that would help people better connect with who you are and what you believe in?

# PART THREE
## MAKE IT LAST

## TEN
# Sustainable By Design

If belonging is the emotional heartbeat of a thriving hospitality business, then sustainability by design is its spine.

Now that you've found your purpose, built something meaningful, and created moments that matter, it's time to make sure it lasts. It isn't about going greener for the sake of a trend. It's about building a business that doesn't break. One that looks after you, your team, your customers, and your future. A business built to go the distance.

Sustainability is often reduced to recycling and carbon footprints. Yes, those matter, but real sustainability goes much deeper. It's about stewardship. It's about creating a business that endures; one that conserves not only environmental but also human energy. A business that supports life and doesn't deplete it. Not just for the sake of the planet, but for the people in your care – and for you.

Once you're leading with purpose, mission, and clarity, you begin to notice that nearly every decision is connected. We need to stop seeing sustainability as a separate project. It's not a badge or a trend. It's not optional. It needs to be embedded in every choice we make. It's about responsibility – leading in a way that doesn't exhaust us or the world around us. It starts with protecting what you already have by cutting the waste that creeps into your time, energy, and resources. It's not an extra task to be done; it's a mindset.

The idea, championed by sustainability experts, of a circular economy is built on the principle that nothing is wasted. Everything has value. Output becomes input. In hospitality, that thinking fits beautifully. We're already wired for it. We thrive on rhythm, routine, and return visits. We train teams through cycles of growth. We create rituals that bring people together. Hospitality, done well, is a circular economy of care.

We can live that out without compromising our people or our planet. Every saved resource, nurtured relationship, and hour used with intention counts. When you build your business on the Five Pillars, you're already reducing waste of energy, attention, money, and morale. You're already making an impact. Even if you don't call it sustainability, that's what it is. Because sustainability isn't just about reducing your carbon footprint or sourcing better ingredients, though that's part of it. It's also about how you lead and protect what matters. It's about how you honour the energy that got you here and use it wisely for the long haul.

## Unsustainable growth

One of the biggest threats to sustainability today isn't found in supply chains or carbon reports. It's in the narratives we've built around growth. Sometimes, what puts sustainability at the greatest risk is the pressure to grow before we're ready.

There's a deeply concerning growth trend among independent hospitality operators. It starts with the first site – full of excitement, drive, and vision. Almost immediately, the conversation shifts to the next site. And the one after that. Many owners talk about building a multi-site operation, inspired by stories of others who started with one location and built an empire.

I'm worried we're not seeing the whole picture. We don't talk enough about the reality behind those success stories. The truth is, most of the operators who scaled that way didn't just work hard and reinvest. More often than not, they had access to serious funding. They got one site working exceptionally well, proved the concept, and then secured investment from a big, faceless fund driven purely by profit rather than by a deeper purpose or belief in the business itself. The investment isn't made because it's meaningful, but because it's scalable. That kind of backing isn't about values or vision; it's about margins. Those operators weren't stretching every penny. They weren't doing it all themselves. They weren't trying to scale while still firefighting. They were, perhaps, even trading integrity for growth.

Meanwhile, independent operators without that backing try to replicate the model. They assume that success lies in doing it well, reinvesting everything, and pushing forwards. They open the second or third site, and they dilute everything: their time, energy, team, and standards. It spreads too thin, too fast. And that is not sustainable.

Instead, I've come to believe that the most powerful thing you can do is pour everything into one site. Grow that site until there are queues before you open, demand outweighs capacity, consistency is second nature, and you know there's still more to give.

You might get bored or crave variety. That's OK. Name that. Acknowledge that the itch to grow could be more about personal satisfaction than business necessity, and then find alternative ways to stretch yourself. Because all too often, opening another site is driven by ego – the need to feel successful. I can tell you from personal experience: it is not always sustainable. I've watched operators learn that lesson the hard way, myself included. If I have any regrets in my career, it's that I over-stretched. I chased more sites, thinking it would bring greater success. It didn't bring more money, just more stress.

One client I worked with had been through a similar experience. He lost everything, including his health, and had to start again. My job was to keep him focused. To remind him that his power now lay in building the best restaurant in the world for his customers. He was full of amazing, creative, and important ideas for the industry, but we made sure he kept channelling that energy into one site. And what happened? He'd never had a more engaged team or more loyal guests. He'd never been in a stronger financial position. Most importantly, he had space in his life for his family and friends. One site. One brilliant business. One thing he could truly love and lead.

You don't have to follow the narrative that growth means scale. You can build something that's right for you. That's the real work. That's what makes it sustainable. Not creating waste. Not burning out. Not chasing growth for the sake of it. Building something that lasts – financially, emotionally, and operationally – and works for the life you want to live.

## Sustainable success means paying yourself first

Leadership is not martyrdom. You are not more committed by being unpaid. If you wouldn't run payroll without paying your team, why is it OK to skip your own wage?

This is one of the hardest truths for many operators to face. But it's also one of the most important. If your business model doesn't allow for you to be paid, it's not viable in the long term, no matter how much customers love your venue or how beautiful it looks on Instagram. Eventually, your energy will run out, resentment will grow, and the whole thing will stop working. Cashflow planning must include you. You are not an optional extra.

I've worked with clients who hadn't paid themselves for years and couldn't look at their personal bank accounts without feeling panicked. Yet, they kept paying suppliers, staff, and rent like clockwork because they felt responsible. If you want to be responsible, start by taking responsibility for your own wellbeing. When you're in survival mode, your decision-making suffers. Your creativity disappears. Your leadership weakens. You lose the very thing you set out to build: freedom.

In *Profit First*, business author Mike Michalowicz outlines a powerful but simple shift: instead of treating profit (and your own wage) as something left over, you build it in first.[30] You take a percentage of every penny earned and allocate it to profit and owner pay before anything else. It's a mindset and values shift, and it works.

This doesn't mean being reckless; it means being intentional. If you can't afford to pay yourself, then your pricing, structure, or overheads need to be reviewed, not your worth.

Ask yourself:

- What is the minimum I need to pay myself to feel safe, confident, and valued?
- What changes need to be made to my pricing, cost structure, or habits to make that possible?
- Where am I accepting a financial standard I'd never ask my team to live on?

Because your financial health isn't just part of your business, it's the spine that holds everything upright.

So, sustainability isn't just a global mission. It's personal. It's local. It starts with each of us doing what is necessary – protecting what we care about. Building something strong enough to last. That means looking after your energy, your team, your customers, and your community. It also means looking after yourself – financially, emotionally, and physically.

When you design for sustainability, and you put systems, standards, and boundaries in place that protect you, you're not being selfish. You're doing the work the world needs more of: work that lasts.

Let this be your reminder: you matter. Your health and income are priorities. This work – the kind that creates belonging, safety, and joy – is too important to burn out. The world needs you in it. Through it all, come back to this: you are the first pebble in the ripple. You are what matters most.

## When I didn't listen

Even with the best plans in place, there will be moments when life gets in the way. There are times when the world shifts, and your business must shift with it. Give yourself a break. Be prepared to pause, adapt, and change plans. That's not failure; that's wisdom.

Let me tell you a story. I'd just got married. I had four kids – one a newborn and the other three diagnosed with autism and ADHD. My mum had recently died. I'd been diagnosed with chronic fatigue, which I chose to ignore. In fact, rather than slowing down, I defiantly set myself a new challenge: to train for a sub-four-hour marathon. I was in the middle of opening a new venue, and I was determined it would succeed. I knew that if I wanted to follow through on everything I'd promised myself, I needed to bring someone in – someone who could hold me to account, challenge my ideas, and guide me.

At our first meeting, the first thing my new business coach said was that I needed to go and see Linda. Linda, who's now a great friend, is a hypnotherapist. At my appointment with her, she asked me why I was there, and I said, 'I don't know.' I explained that I was about to go on my honeymoon – two weeks in Mauritius, by the pool. My idea of a dream holiday had always been finding somewhere to walk up a mountain, so sitting by a pool was completely out of my comfort zone. But it's what you do on a honeymoon, isn't it? So, that's what we were doing.

I was feeling anxious because we were going somewhere so beautiful and expensive, and I was worried I wouldn't be able to relax. Linda asked me to visualise another time in my life when I had felt truly relaxed. Nothing came to mind. That was the start of my education in self-compassion, and it had been a long time coming.

The previous ten years had taken their toll, both professionally and personally, physically and emotionally. I'd left a marriage and walked away from the business I'd built from scratch to get a clean break from my ex-husband, who was also my business partner. At the time, I was fuelled by youth, energy, and blind optimism. I chose what felt like the simplest path: start again.

I had no home, no income, no business – just three children under eight, all of whom were later diagnosed as neurodivergent. What followed was the most painful, relentless decade of my life. Divorce. Rebuilding. Raising young kids. A new home. A new relationship. A traumatic childbirth that almost killed me. Losing my mum. Losing momentum in my business. A flood that forced us to close for weeks. Riots outside the venue that emptied the streets and deterred customers. A diagnosis of chronic fatigue that I refused to acknowledge.

Still, I kept going. Still, I kept building. Still, I kept pushing forwards. By the time I ended up in Linda's office, asking to be hypnotised so I could relax on a beach, I hadn't truly paused for over a decade. I didn't know how to stop or rest. I didn't know what it meant to be gentle with myself.

In that moment, when I was unable to recall a single time I had ever felt fully relaxed, I realised something needed to change, not in how I ran my business, but in how I treated myself.

## The superpower that became my kryptonite

I've always felt lucky that I don't really get stressed. I thrive when things are busy, and I'm at my best in a crisis. When everyone else is flailing, I can stay calm, assess the situation, prioritise, and make things happen. It's one of the reasons I've always been so drawn to hospitality – the constant variety and need for problem-solving. I see it in many of us who have stayed as operators. We love making sense of the chaos.

Now, my superpower has become my kryptonite. Unbeknownst to me, while I thought I was getting by, my body had been keeping the score. When my youngest daughter was born, I lost two and a half litres of blood. A year later, I still felt awful. It got to the point where I could barely get out of bed. Even a slow stroll to the shops required a nap afterwards. Working was tough. It was difficult to concentrate. Of course, like many leaders, I masked the issue. I didn't let anyone know how hard it had become.

After years of tests, I was finally diagnosed with chronic fatigue. I remember walking out of the doctor's room thinking, 'Not me, no, that's not me.'

## Rebuilding from the inside out

Little by little, I worked on rebuilding my stamina. Slow walks around the block until, eventually, those walks became runs, and I felt strong enough to train. And train I did. I ran that marathon. I crossed the line at 03:58:58, sixty-two seconds faster than my goal. It was a personal victory, but I pushed so hard to prove I was OK that I missed what my body was trying to tell me. While I might have beaten the clock that day, I lost a lot in the process. Having pushed myself physically harder than ever before, I began experiencing frightening neurological symptoms: tingling sensations throughout my body and permanent nerve damage. Still, I didn't slow down. It took me a long time to forgive myself for that.

I wasn't just running businesses; I had a full life away from work, too. This was all happening against the backdrop of my children going through some of the hardest, most heartbreaking times of their lives. I was showing up every day: smiling at customers, keeping my cool with staff, trying to lead with strength and steadiness. Behind the scenes, I was up at 5.30am and still awake past 11pm, nursing one or another of my children through the kind of turmoil that comes with a sensitive, overwhelmed mind, and suffering so profound it was almost unbearable to witness.

I saw so many specialists over the years, trying to get answers and find a silver bullet that would allow me to continue at my current pace. I'd like to tell you that I now fully accept the diagnosis. It's been confirmed by every specialist I've seen. But the truth is, I still don't want to accept that I can't push through.

The reality is, I've done permanent physical damage. If I'm not careful – if I don't manage things daily – I can make myself so unwell that all the things I love about this wonderful, messy life have to be put on hold. Days, and sometimes weeks or even months, are lost to recovery. My body is now in charge, and it's louder than my head, which still believes I'm invincible. If I push too hard, my body will tell me, and it won't whisper any more.

When Linda later circled back to her initial question, asking if I could name a single moment I'd felt truly relaxed, I still drew a blank. She asked me to say something nice about myself. Again, I froze. The words wouldn't come. I had only ever taken on board the negative things others had said. I knew deep down that I was a compassionate and caring boss, but others had seen me differently. I had been trolled and vilified so many times throughout my career that, honestly, I felt incredibly lonely. It was a genuine surprise when people described me as 'nice'.

The most extraordinary thing about my story is that it's not unusual. In fact, it's no more remarkable than the stories I hear from operators every day. This industry is full of people holding it together while everything around them unravels; those who lead with their hearts, take on too much, and quietly carry an emotional load most outsiders will never understand.

## Self-compassion is strategy

Self-compassion is looking after yourself first. It's recognising that being kind to others and being a good leader only work if it comes from within – from your internal dialogue, the time and patience you give yourself, and protecting your energy.

Now, I meditate. I gently exercise every day and resist the urge to push myself with a long run. I take time to sit down. I find rubbish TV to help me switch off. I go to bed early. I try to eat well. I even use affirmations on occasion. I listen when I receive good feedback, and I reward myself weekly for my wins, no matter how small. I take breaks. I still find it hard to relax when I'm not at work, but I've learned how to keep myself gently occupied while still giving myself space to rest. It's a skill.

Life is hard and messy. It's never perfect. We are all doing our best. You will not build a stand-out, successful business; create a team that trusts you, shares your mission and vision, and feels safe under your leadership; or build a community of customers who truly love what you do, unless you put on your own oxygen mask first.

Each of the Five Pillars in this book – setting high standards, standing out, defining your identity, building belonging, and telling your story – relies on your ability to lead yourself first.

Before you close this book and dive back into your business, pause and consider:

- When did you last feel truly rested?

- What would change if you treated your own wellbeing as a core part of your business plan – as a necessity, not a luxury?

- What would happen if you decided that your energy, clarity, and health weren't things you needed to sacrifice, but instead were the very things that make your business thrive?

Let this be your first act of leadership.

## You've built the framework, now live it

You've done the deep work. You've faced the real problems behind the noise. You've explored your values, your story, and your customers. You've reconnected with why this matters. Now, you have a framework to guide you forwards – one that's rooted in your reality, not someone else's.

The Five Pillars of Stand Out Hospitality are not just concepts; they are your practical, emotional, and strategic anchors. They help you simplify decisions, find clarity, and act with purpose.

1. **Set High Standards:** Lead with consistency, clarity, and care.

2. **Stand Out:** Tune out the noise. Own your niche. Be unforgettable to the right people.

3. **Define Your Identity:** Be purpose driven. Know who you are and whom you serve.

4. **Build Belonging:** Create strong emotional connections with your customers and team.

5. **Tell A Great Story:** Share your 'why'. Let people in. Use storytelling to build visibility, trust, and loyalty.

You don't need to do everything at once. This isn't a checklist or another source of pressure to be perfect. This is your rhythm. Your compass. Your way back when things get tough.

Start small. Pick a pillar and make one decision today that brings you back into alignment. Whether it's how you show up for your team, a change to your menu, a story you tell on Instagram, or a brave 'no' to a customer who's not your tribe, it counts. You will forget and return, drift and reset. That's what leadership involves. These pillars are reminders, not rules. Tools, not tasks. A mindset, not a destination.

You've built this. Now live it. Because the moment you decide to lead with purpose, reconnect with your truth, and serve from the inside out, you've already made the shift. You're not just running a business. You're creating somewhere that matters.

## It takes a village

You might be the leader, the one who sets the tone, but you're not meant to do this alone. No business thrives in isolation. Even the most iconic venues – those we all admire – aren't built by one person. They are co-created, shaped by the people who show up day after day and pour themselves into it. Your team, customers, suppliers, mentors, designers, coaches, and cheerleaders. The friends who challenge you. The strangers who believe in you. The community that shares your values. Hospitality has always been about people, and so is business growth.

It takes a village to build something special. To hold you up on the hard days and remind you of your purpose when the noise gets loud. To challenge you to stay brave when you want to hide. To celebrate with you when you win. To help you dream bigger than you thought you could. A community doesn't just cheer you on. It shapes you. It keeps you honest. It makes your ideas better. It's where momentum is born.

So, if you've done the work and built the framework, don't stop there. Surround yourself with people who understand. People who believe as you do. People who will keep showing up, long after the buzz dies down. When you invest in community, you don't just grow your business; you create a place where ideas flow. A place where courage builds, belonging begins, and success becomes something we share.

## Summary

This chapter reminded you that sustainability isn't a project, it's a mindset. It's not just about carbon footprints or recycling targets. It's about building a business that holds you, instead of hollowing you out.

You saw that real sustainability starts with protecting your own energy, paying yourself properly, and designing a business that works for the long haul and not just the next season. Because when growth comes too fast, or from the wrong place, it can cost you everything. You don't have to follow someone else's blueprint. You can build one brilliant site and let that be enough.

You heard what happens when we ignore the warning signs. How the pressure to prove ourselves can lead to burnout, illness, and loss, and how easily we can become the last person on our own priority list. You also saw what changes when you start from care. When you honour your time, health, and boundaries without apology. Because sustainability isn't selfish. It's what allows you to keep going and create the kind of business and life that actually fits.

This chapter asked you to pause and stop chasing more for the sake of it. Remember: your energy is precious. Your presence matters. You are the first ripple. If this business is going to last, it must also last for you.

# Conclusion: Let It Be You

You've read the book and reflected. Now, it's time to begin. Don't start with a grand relaunch, a new concept, or a marketing plan. Start with you – feeling more grounded, clearer, and ready to lead in a way that feels true.

## Start where you are

We began this book by reminding ourselves in Chapter One why hospitality matters, not just as an industry, but as a human need. A place for connection, belonging, and meaning. A thousand years of shared stories and standing shoulder to shoulder. You saw how the work you do now is part of that legacy, and how those small moments still matter more than ever.

In Chapter Two, we acknowledged the truth: this industry is hard. Brilliant, but brutal. We looked honestly at the reality facing independent operators today. The external pressures, the uncertainty, and the way it all lands squarely on your shoulders. In that context, we focused on customers, the first of ninety-nine problems facing operators today. As customers' needs have changed, businesses that stand out emotionally, not just operationally, are the ones they come back to.

In Chapter Three, we turned to teams. People hold everything together, but holding them in turn takes more energy than ever. We explored how expectations have shifted: this generation is raising the bar because they're no longer willing to accept what came before. When it comes to leading well, you saw that your presence, not just your process, is what people respond to most.

Then, in Chapter Four, we looked at the weight you carry: the emotional load, risk, and reality of trying to do it all. The truth is, this isn't just a job. It's your time, reputation, future, and peace of mind, all wrapped up in one relentless responsibility. We discussed what overwhelm really feels like. We explored why looking after yourself isn't optional; it's the foundation on which everything else stands.

We learned about the seven most common mistakes that hospitality operators make. Not to judge, but to reflect. We saw how easy it is to fall into patterns when the pressure is on and, more importantly, how stand-out businesses do things differently. Not by doing more, but by doing less, better. From there, you were introduced to the Five Pillars of Stand Out Hospitality – your anchor points, compass, and daily rhythm. A way of thinking that reflects values, clarity, and purpose.

We started with **Set High Standards** in Chapter Five, because how you do things matters. You explored what it means to lead from the inside out – to hold the line, set the tone, and deliver with clarity, consistency, and care. High standards aren't about control; they're about pride. The quiet kind that lives in the details. The culture you create starts with the example you set. You are the first pebble in the pond. When you show up with purpose, it ripples outwards to your team and customers, influencing how people feel when they walk through the door. That's what real leadership looks like. It starts with you.

Next, came **Stand Out** in Chapter Six. In a world full of noise, being different is your greatest strength. You looked at how to stop blending in and instead claim what sets you apart by making grounded, confident decisions. You saw that trying to be everything to everyone is exhausting. You explored how to tune out the pressure and focus on what only you can do, and how owning your difference allows you to become a beacon for the right people.

In Chapter Seven, **Define Your Identity**, you went deeper. You looked honestly at what drives you – your values, purpose, and deeper motivation – and how to build a business that reflects that from the inside out. You saw that being purpose-driven isn't a luxury; it's the key to building something that works. Having a strong sense of direction isn't just for you; it's what your team and your customers need. People are looking for a mission-driven leader to follow. When you know who you are and what you stand for, they feel it. Decisions get easier. Direction gets sharper.

From that focus, something powerful happens. You stop trying to serve everyone and start designing for the people you're really here for. The right customers – those who energise your work and your team loves serving. You learned how to build a business that truly understands them, in which every product, system, and standard is created with their needs in mind. Instead of chasing approval, you become the best in the world for the people who matter most.

Then, in Chapter Eight, we explored **Build Belonging** because this work is emotional. People don't come back just for food and drink. They come back for how a place makes them feel, for the welcome and the sense that they are understood. You saw that not all customers or team members are equal, and that it's OK to let some people go because this isn't about trying to be all things to all people. It's about designing for the right ones and building something that works

## CONCLUSION: LET IT BE YOU

for them. You used the customer map to gain clarity about who they are and how to shape every product and standard around what they need. Because when someone feels like your place was made for them, they stay. They bring their friends. They become your biggest fans. This isn't about transaction; it's about connection. That's how loyalty is earned and not bought. That's how you stop chasing and start attracting. That's how you build not only a business but a tribe.

In Chapter Nine, **Tell a Great Story**, you brought it all together. Hospitality is where stories happen. You're not just serving meals; you're creating memories. You looked at how everything you do becomes part of someone's story: how the room feels, how the team shows up, and the way the moments land. You realised that marketing isn't a separate task; it's baked into the experience. It's how people talk about you when you're not in the room. You learned that a story isn't a trick; it's trust. It's how people feel something real. Because customers don't fall in love with logos. They fall in love with people – with founders who care, teams who connect, and places that feel like they were built just for them.

When you lead with your own story – showing up with confidence, conviction, and something real to say – people don't just remember you; they root for you. They carry your message. They bring others with them because great stories spread. When the story is true and the feeling is right, magic happens. You're not just running a business; you're creating something people want to belong to. And the story is how they find you.

The Five Pillars don't ask you to become someone else; they encourage you to be more yourself. They're not a checklist; they're a way to lead with confidence, intention, and integrity. They act as a touchstone for the days when everything feels noisy. Building a stand-out business isn't about chasing someone else's definition of success. It's about creating something that feels right from the inside, and using that lens to shape how you hire, serve, market, and grow. It doesn't just simplify decisions; it makes them feel more honest, better aligned, and more you.

Finally, in Chapter Ten, we brought it all together with sustainability. Not sustainability as a buzzword or a branding tactic, but as a way of working that doesn't burn you out. A business model that protects your time, income, and ability to keep showing up. One that supports your team, customers, and personal life. Because real success isn't about how fast you grow; it's about whether you can keep going. We looked at the true cost of continually pushing forwards, of expanding when the foundations aren't ready, and treating exhaustion as a badge of honour.

We challenged the pressure to scale for its own sake. Because sustainability isn't just environmental; it's deeply personal. It's about building something that holds you up, not hollows you out. Something that pays you well, gives you space to breathe, and still feels good at the end of the week. When your business is built with that kind of purpose, everything else falls into place. Environmental goals stop being add-ons or afterthoughts and become the natural result of a business that values people, energy, time, and trust. That's not compromise; that's what win–win really looks like.

Now, start where you are – with whatever energy, perspective, or courage this book has stirred in you. Maybe it gave voice to something you've always felt. Perhaps it made you braver. Maybe it just reminded you that you're not alone. Whatever you choose next, remember: this work matters. You've built more than a business – you've built a place where people feel something and stories begin. That is no small thing. Let that be your North Star. When things get loud again, you know exactly where to return to.

## The world we're building

The Kith & Kin vision is a thriving, values-led independent hospitality sector where no one feels alone and everyone can find where they belong. Our mission is to help make that world possible: to show independent hospitality leaders that their greatest competitive advantage is belonging, creating the kind of places people never want to leave. Places where people feel seen, connected, and proud to be part of.

I still carry the scars of doing all this alone, and I don't want anyone, especially those still doing the work and pouring in all their passion and heart, to feel that same loneliness. As Rutger Bregman writes in *Humankind*: 'We are evolutionarily programmed to share, to cooperate, and to learn from one another.'[31] I want to be here to offer a hand, an ear, and to share everything I've learned, so others don't have to learn the hard way.

## Why chains still dominate

The world I envision is possible. Independent hospitality can – and does – stand out, even in a landscape dominated by big chains and lookalike venues. Those businesses only manage to dominate the high street for two reasons.

The first reason is financial. Chains have deep pockets and big investors. But just because you see them everywhere doesn't mean those businesses are doing any better than you. Some of those chains operate venues that don't make a profit, but their presence boosts brand recognition in that area. As stand-alone businesses, they're being propped up by the success of other sites or by the deep pockets of their investors. Independent hospitality can't play that game. We don't have the luxury of running at break-even or at a loss, because our businesses have to be more than just a façade.

The second reason is customer behaviour. As we've discussed many times in this book, customers crave consistency. These days, they're more cautious with how they spend their money and their time. So, when they're choosing where to eat out or stay overnight, they often default to the familiar chain. Not because it's the best, but because it feels safer. They know they're probably sacrificing quality, and certainly heart, but that 'almost good enough' feeling is better than the frustration of making a bad call. When an independent hospitality venue fails to meet expectations, the disappointment hits harder.

The truth is, trying somewhere new without a trusted recommendation can feel like a game of roulette. In a world full of samey chains, the devil you know offers the easy choice.

## Why independents can win

There isn't much we can do to level the playing field when it comes to investment and money, but we absolutely can stand out to the customer. In fact, we've explored the framework that will help your independent business do exactly that. This is where our biggest challenge becomes our greatest strength.

We're at the coalface. We see the world in real time. We're small, agile, and deeply connected to the day-to-day aspects that make us vulnerable, but we know our businesses inside out – our strengths, our weaknesses – and we adapt quickly. Independent hospitality is where real innovation happens. It's where the creativity in this industry lives.

When lockdown hit and the world was searching for hope amid the trauma, it was the independent hospitality sector that stepped up. We saw leaders roll up their sleeves and dive into community support – delivering groceries to neighbours, cooking for NHS teams, keeping people fed and connected when everything else shut down.

It wasn't just care; it was creativity, too. We supplied industrial-scale home cocktail kits, restaurant-quality meal boxes, bake-at-home pizza and pastry deliveries, and finish-at-home Sunday roasts. We transformed car parks into covered courtyards and designed extraordinary outdoor dining experiences. We embraced new technology that not only helped us reopen but also advanced the whole industry by a decade.

We are open, curious, and creative. We are entrepreneurial to the core. Even in the hardest of times, we step forwards and find ways to make our corner of the world better – for our teams, customers, and communities. This is an unbelievably exciting industry, filled with deeply caring, endlessly inventive, and genuinely interesting people.

CONCLUSION: LET IT BE YOU

After all, when is a pub not a pub? When it's a post office, a deli, a shop, a community centre, a food bank, a parcel drop-off point, a meeting room, or even a pop-up gallery. This has always been the heart of our industry; we were never just about serving food and drink.

The truth is, the world where independents outperform the chains already exists. You've built it. Now it's time to do more and bring others with us. The world we are building is a thriving, values-led independent hospitality sector where everyone feels at home and finds where they belong.

## Before you go

(A note from me to you.)

This book is about how to build a hospitality business that truly stands out. Not through gimmicks or grand gestures, but by being clear about who you are, whom you serve, and why it all matters. By doing the deep work that helps you lead with clarity, build emotional loyalty, and tell a story that people want to be part of.

It's about becoming the kind of business that people don't just visit, but they fall in love with. The kind that stays in their hearts. The kind that matters.

That kind of business doesn't build itself; it takes leadership. It takes someone brave enough to take responsibility – not just for standards and systems, but for the energy, clarity, and culture that defines the whole experience. It takes someone who is willing to go first.

There's a parable that my gran had pinned up in her kitchen:

> 'Four people were asked to do something important: Everybody, Somebody, Anybody, and Nobody. Everybody thought Somebody would do it. Anybody could have done it. But Nobody did.'

Don't let that be your story. Let it be you. Be the one who sets the tone. Be the one who decides that's enough of chasing, of noise, and of trying to be all things to all people. Be the one who builds a business with purpose and heart. A business that welcomes the right people, upholds its standards, and creates real belonging for your team, your customers, and yourself. That's the bravery the industry needs.

Do it with kindness. The kind that starts with how you treat yourself, because you can't lead from a place of exhaustion. You can't create a culture of care if you're constantly running on empty. Self-compassion isn't a soft option; it's essential. It's the oxygen mask that lets you keep going. Be kind to yourself. Forgive the mistakes. Notice the wins. Celebrate the moments that matter.

Then, look up, because you don't have to do this alone. It takes personal responsibility to lead, but it takes a village to thrive. The most resilient hospitality businesses are those that don't try to do it all alone. They build communities around themselves, including their team, customers, suppliers, and supporters. That's what makes the difference.

That's what Kith & Kin is here for. To be the place where you find others who care as much as you do. Where your voice matters. Where you feel seen. Where you belong.

Remember this: you only fail when you give up.

Take these final thoughts with you. You don't need to be perfect. You don't need to be fearless. You just need to start. Hospitality isn't just a job; it's a stage for human connection. It's where memories are made and stories begin. You're the one who makes that happen. Be the one who dares. Be the one who leads with heart. Be the one who sets the tone. Be the one who shows up.

Let it be you.

# Next Steps

If *Stand Out Hospitality* struck a chord, it's because you care deeply about doing things the right way. About building something meaningful and making hospitality feel human again.

That's why we built **Kith & Kin**, a values-led community and support network for independent hospitality people who want to lead with clarity, grow with integrity, and surround themselves with others who understand.

Whether you run a pub, café, hotel, restaurant or street food brand, Kith & Kin is here to help you move from overwhelmed to aligned; from doing it all alone, to doing it together.

This book is just the beginning. The next steps are:

- **Download the templates, customer avatar worksheet, and other free tools** at https://kithkinhospitality.co.uk/book-resources
- **Listen to our podcast, *Kith & Kin Hospitality*,** which relates real stories from the hospitality industry: https://open.spotify.com/show/1j6dBBhN2BoSbOCXITfkTO
- **Join a free webinar** to hear about what others are building
- **Book onto our live event** and shape your next chapter
- **Join the Kith & Kin community** to find where you belong and stay connected to people who lift you up, challenge your thinking, and help uphold your high standards

This is where loyalty begins. This is how stand-out businesses grow. This is your invitation. Head to kithkinhospitality.co.uk. Everything you need is there.

Let's build something that lasts. Together.

# Notes

1. Charnwood Borough Council, 'Thomas Cook', Discover Charnwood, www.discovercharnwood.co.uk/thomas-cook, accessed 24 June 2025
2. Campaign for Real Ale (CAMRA), 'Porch House, Stow-on-the-Wold' (CAMRA WhatPub), https://camra.org.uk/pubs/porch-house-stow-on-the-wold-162432, accessed 24 June 2025
3. El-Beih, Y, 'How coffee forever changed Britain' (BBC Travel, 2020), www.bbc.co.uk/travel/article/20201119-how-coffee-forever-changed-britain, accessed 24 June 2025
4. Maslow, AH, *Motivation and Personality*, 3rd edition (Harper & Row, 1987)
5. Guidara, W, *Unreasonable Hospitality: The remarkable power of giving people more than they expect* (Optimism Press, 2022)

6   Robbins, T, 'Discover the 6 human needs', Tony Robbins' Blog, www.tonyrobbins.com/blog/do-you-need-to-feel-significant?srsltid=AfmBOopTCjOhyd8qIKWbWvCLlm3GXT8nrXE1tWVSM94PH6SUzb17LYSB, accessed 24 June 2025

7   Oldenburg, R, *The Great Good Place: Cafés, coffee shops, bookstores, bars, hair salons, and other hangouts at the heart of a community* (Marlowe & Company, 1999)

8   UK Government, 'Licensing Act 2003', www.legislation.gov.uk/ukpga/2003/17/contents, accessed 24 June 2025

9   Smith, D, *Delia Smith's Complete Cookery Course* (BBC Books, 2001)

10  Bennetts, R, 'IAS briefing paper: Use of alcohol as a loss-leader' (Institute of Alcohol Studies, 3 June 2008), www.ias.org.uk/uploads/pdf/IAS%20reports/lossleading.pdf, accessed 25 June 2025

11  Talbot, D, *The Sober Myth: Are young adults really a generation of non-drinkers?* (Drinkaware, 2023), www.drinkaware.co.uk/research/research-and-evaluation-reports/the-sober-myth-are-young-adults-really-a-generation-of-non-drinkers, accessed 25 June 2025

12  Barclays, *10 Years of Spend: What can the last decade of consumer spending tell us about the next?* (Barclays, June 2025), https://home.barclays/insights/2025/06/10-years-of-spend, accessed 25 June 2025

# NOTES

13 Office for National Statistics (ONS), 'Consumer trends, UK: October to December 2024' (Office for National Statistics, 28 March 2025), www.ons.gov.uk/economy/nationalaccounts/satelliteaccounts/bulletins/consumertrends/octobertodecember2024, accessed 24 June 2025

14 The Burnt Chef Project, 'About', The Burnt Chef Project, www.theburntchefproject.com/about, accessed 24 June 2025

15 SanaMente, 'Next generation workforce; from frustrations to flourishing', Strive with SanaMente, www.strive-online.co.uk/strive-podcasts, accessed 24 June 2025

16 Roosevelt, T, 'Citizenship in a republic', speech delivered at the Sorbonne, Paris, 23 April 1910 (The American Presidency Project, University of California, Santa Barbara), www.presidency.ucsb.edu/documents/address-the-sorbonne-paris-france-citizenship-republic, accessed 25 June 2025

17 Godin, S, *The Dip: A little book that teaches you when to quit (and when to stick)* (Portfolio, 2007)

18 Sinek, S, *Start with Why: How great leaders inspire everyone to take action* (Portfolio, 2009)

19 Scott, S, *Fierce Conversations: Achieving success at work and in life, one conversation at a time* (Piatkus, 2004)

20 Godin, S, *The Practice: Shipping creative work* (Portfolio, 2020)

21 Meyer, D, *Setting the Table: The transforming power of hospitality in business* (HarperCollins, 2006)

22 Rohn, J, *The Treasury of Quotes* (Made for Success Publishing, 2011)
23 Bregman, R, *Humankind: A hopeful history* (Bloomsbury Publishing, 2020)
24 United Nations, *World Population Prospects 2024: Summary of results* (United Nations, July 2024), https://population.un.org/wpp/assets/Files/WPP2024_Summary-of-Results.pdf, accessed 25 June 2025
25 Bitsy's Emporium of Awesome, www.bitsysemporium.com, accessed 24 June 2025
26 Rustic Kitchen & Deli, www.rustickitchendeli.com, accessed 24 June 2025
27 Bower, T, and Harding, L, *What's the Story? Hash Brown Glory* (podcast), available on Spotify, https://creators.spotify.com/pod/profile/whats-the-story-hash-brow, accessed 15 July 2025
28 Neumeier, M, *The Brand Gap: How to bridge the distance between business strategy and design* (New Riders, 2005)
29 The Secret Pub Company, 'Awards and recognition' (The Railway Lowdham), https://railwaylowdham.co.uk/awards-recognition, accessed 24 June 2025
30 Michalowicz, M, *Profit First: Transform your business from a cash-eating monster to a money-making machine* (Portfolio, 2017)
31 Bregman, R, *Humankind: A hopeful history* (Bloomsbury Publishing, 2020)

# Further Reading

Brown, B, *Dare to Lead: Brave Work. Tough Conversations. Whole Hearts.* (Vermilion, 2018)

Canfield, J, *The Success Principles: How to get from where you are to where you want to be* (HarperCollins, 2005)

Godin, S, *Purple Cow: Transform your business by being remarkable* (Portfolio, 2003)

Godin, S, *Tribes: We need you to lead us* (Portfolio, 2008)

Higgins, S, *Power of Love Leadership: 7 proven strategies to drive success, maximise results and inspire compassion and trust* (SRA Books, 2020)

Kishimi, I, and Koga F, *The Courage to Be Disliked: How to free yourself, change your life and achieve real happiness* (Allen & Unwin, 2018)

Robbins, T, *Awaken the Giant Within: How to take immediate control of your mental, emotional, physical and financial destiny!* (Free Press, 1991)

Schwartz, B, *The Paradox of Choice: Why more is less* (Harper Perennial, 2004)

# Acknowledgements

First, of course, my family, for being the place where I belong. I'm incredibly lucky to have you. You teach me something new every day, and I feel that theme of learning from those who went before me, through me, to the next generation in everything I do.

I don't say it often enough, but I've learned so much from my sisters. We've shared experiences, but you've both walked your own paths, and there's wisdom in that.

To my children, nieces and nephews: you're growing up in a different world, and you've opened my eyes to things I should have seen sooner and things I never knew were possible. So much of your insight has been channelled into this book. I love you all, and thank you.

To my gloriously nerdy dad: I still roll my eyes when you share obscure details (like Thomas Cook's first trip from Leicester to Loughborough), but we both know I'm secretly listening. I see that same eyeroll when I share my own nerdy facts with my kids, and I know they're secretly listening, too. Dad, I've been incredibly fortunate to have parents who always made me believe I could do anything. You and Mum were quietly disruptive in your own ways – questioning the rules, challenging the status quo – and that gave me the freedom to think differently, too.

You didn't just support me; you actively encouraged me. From that first conversation, aged twenty-two, in a seaside café when I said I wanted to open my own place until now, building Kith & Kin, you've been there. Guiding me, mentoring me, and, occasionally, acting as my unauthorised overdraft. Thank you. Truly. None of this would have been possible without your quiet optimism, unwavering belief, and the steady confidence you've always had in me.

To my husband: Belle, and Beau x

To all my friends, both those who are still here and those who have moved on, you were and are my tribe. Thank you for being part of the journey.

## ACKNOWLEDGEMENTS

Thank you to the early readers of this book. At times, I didn't know if I could write it, but your thoughtful, compassionate feedback helped shape this into something real, relevant, and (I hope) meaningful for the hospitality industry.

To my publishers and everyone at Rethink, thank you for being such an incredible team to work with. It is a real privilege to have experts who have your back. I am deeply grateful for the care you put into every stage, and for making the journey feel smooth and manageable. I don't envy the complexity of your work, but I am truly appreciative of the way you do it.

To the Kith & Kin community: leaving the front line of hospitality to build something for those who are still in it wasn't easy, but I have been lifted by how you embraced the vision. Kith & Kin was never about me; it has always been about you. It's a privilege to continue serving this industry by serving you.

The same applies to the wider ecosystem: the brilliant community of suppliers, creatives, freelancers, coaches, and allies who lift the industry every day. Your contribution matters more than you know.

To every team member I've worked with, thank you. You helped build and shape each of those special places.

Thank you to my customers, especially those who loved those places more than I did. It was a huge privilege.

Finally, to you – the reader, the leader, the owner, the builder, the one still standing – thank you for doing the work you do. I wrote this for you.

# The Author

Cassie Davison is a hospitality leader, business coach, and the founder of Kith & Kin, a movement for independent hospitality operators and their wider community. Built on the belief that belonging is independent hospitality's greatest competitive advantage, Kith & Kin brings together those at the heart of the industry and those who serve it, united by a commitment to doing things differently.

With over thirty years in the industry, Cassie has built, grown, and led award-winning pubs, cafés, fine-dining restaurants, and even festivals from the ground up. She's known for combining real-world experience with strategic insight, helping hospitality leaders reconnect with their purpose, lead with clarity, and build businesses that thrive.

Cassie holds an MBA and has earned over twenty-five business and hospitality industry awards, but her greatest accolade is having stood exactly where her readers stand – on the floor and in the back office, in the thick of it. Her coaching is direct, grounded, and rooted in lived experience, designed to help owners grow their business without losing sight of themselves.

Through her podcast, Kith & Kin, and her book *Stand Out Hospitality*, Cassie is shaping a new narrative for the sector – one that values emotional connection as much as commercial success and redefines what it means to lead in independent hospitality in a fast-changing world.

She lives in the UK with her family, her cat, and her dog. She loves a good oat flat white and still believes that hospitality is one of the most powerful forces for good in the world.

🌐 kithkinhospitality.co.uk

f www.facebook.com/kithkin2020

in www.linkedin.com/in/cassiedavison1

📷 @kith_kin_hospitality

www.ingramcontent.com/pod-product-compliance
Lightning Source LLC
Chambersburg PA
CBHW011404210526
45464CB00010B/3040